"Let Rosemary Williams lead you on your personal money journey as you read A Woman's Book of Money & Spiritual Vision. You will begin by identifying the often confusing messages you received in childhood about money. As you travel through the pages of this book, you will begin to understand your feelings about such issues as abundance, scarcity, earning, investing, spending, and giving. Throughout your journey, you'll compare these messages and feelings about money with your spiritual beliefs. By the end of the trip, you will be ready to map out a plan to align your actions with your values. You will advance from vulnerability to possibility, and ultimately achieve 'a fuller version of womanhood and personhood.'

Bon voyage!"

—*Andrea Kaminski, Executive Director,*
Women's Philanthropy Institute

A Woman's Book of Money & Spiritual Vision

A Woman's Book of Money & Spiritual Vision

Putting Your Financial Values into Spiritual Perspective

by Rosemary Williams

with Joanne Kabak

Innisfree
Press, Inc.

*A call to the
deep heart's core*

Published by Innisfree Press, Inc.
136 Roumfort Road
Philadelphia, PA 19119

Visit our website at www.InnisfreePress.com

Cover and book design by Hugh Duffy, PhD Design, Carney's Point, NJ

Library of Congress Cataloging-in-Publication Data
    Williams, Rosemary, date
        A woman's book of money & spiritual vision : putting your financial values
    into spiritual perspective / by Rosemary Williams ; with Joanne Kabak.
            p. cm.
        Includes bibliographical references and index.
        ISBN 1-880913-44-5
        1. Women—Finance, Personal. 2. Finance, Personal—Religious
    aspects—Christianity. I. Title: Woman's book of money and spiritual vision.
        I. Kabak, Joanne, date. III. Title.
HG179.W5343   2001
332.024'042—dc21   2001024094

The author gratefully acknowledges permission to reprint the following:

"I Tremble on the Edge of a Maybe" by Ted Loder, from *Guerrillas of Grace: Prayers for the Battle.*
Copyright © 1984 by Innisfree Press. Reprinted by permission.

"A Psalm for Midwives" by Miriam Therese Winter, from *Woman Witness* (Crossroads, 1992).
Copyright © 1992 by Medical Mission Sisters. Reprinted by permission.

"Birther of Dreams" by Ruth Halvorson. Reprinted by permission.

To my dear friend, mentor, and role model, Dr. Ida F. Davidoff, who has discussed the various ideas in this book with me for years. I will always cherish you, our friendship, and the many provocative discussions we have shared.

(I started to write this book on August 30,1999, which coincidentally was Dr. Davidoff's 96th birthday. —Rosemary Williams)

CONTENTS

Part Two

Chapter 3: UNCOVERING YOUR MONEY FACTS & FEELINGS

Chapter 4: CREATING ALIGNMENT

Part Three
CHAPTER 5: DREAM ON

Chapter 6: YOUR ACTION PLAN

Gratitudes

In writing this book, I am especially grateful for the wisdom and grace that is not of my own doing, but that comes from the workings of the Spirit of God. There are many people who have been directly involved in this project and to whom I feel much gratitude. I want to thank my collaborator, Joanne Kabak, who put my ideas into the written word; Marcia Broucek, my publisher and editor, who has supported and shaped this project from its inception; and Marjory Bankson and Ruth Butler who provided a very special kind of listening and encouragement. I also want to give my thanks to those who opened their hearts and let their stories be told.

In addition, I am a very grateful to the many, many people who have influenced this book. It would be impossible to name them all for they include my family, friends, colleagues, clients, co-workers, and fellow seekers who have supported me throughout my life. I look forward to continuing on the journey with them, and with all those who join in the search for the alignment of their financial life with their spiritual vision.

A New Beginning

It starts with a story . . .

This book is a very different look at money. It is not just about organizing your finances better... though you will learn how to do that. Nor is it about ways to contribute more for the good of others... though you will surely be encouraged to do so.

This "workshop in a book" is designed especially for women who would like to change their way of looking at money—from a material base to a spiritual base, from consumption to generosity, from bettering their own world to bettering everyone's world.

Money and spirituality are not mutually exclusive. I believe there is a spiritual dimension to money that can be tapped for your benefit—and for global benefit—and this book is directed toward that end. This is a book about awareness, acceptance, and action. It starts with understanding your personal financial facts and uncovering the feelings that these facts bring up. And it continues with an ongoing alignment of those facts and feelings with your core desires and intentions.

"There's no doubt in my mind that a new age is dawning. I've decided to live as freely and fully as possible, trusting that my individual actions will help move us toward this new awareness."

—a woman in her thirties who lives in New England, from Miriam Therese Winter's DEFECTING IN PLACE

There are some points along the road of your life where your financial and spiritual aspects touch each other in a very direct way. At other times, they run parallel to one another. But they are never far apart, even if your awareness is not specifically drawn to them.

Perhaps if I share part of my story with you, I can illustrate what I mean. As is true for many women, pain and necessity have often been my teachers and have forced me to change. During a time of downsizing and bank mergers in New England in the early nineties, I lost my job as a banker. I opened a financial planning practice on my own and later joined a friend who was also a financial planner. At this time I was introduced to the Ministry of Money and the Women's Perspective, an ecumenical organization that works with the subject of money as it connects to spirituality and stewardship.

The idea of seeing money through a spiritual lens was compelling to me. I went to a few Ministry of Money workshops, volunteered as a financial planner with this organization, and became more and more interested in the work they were doing. The director invited me to accompany him and a few board members to Haiti for three days. I asked, "Why?" He replied, "I'd like to introduce you to some people there and to what we are doing."

Sometimes a simple invitation can change your life.

That simple invitation changed my life and became the inspiration for my future work. I am now director of the Women's Perspective and deeply committed to creating workshops for women and sustaining the women's programs we have initiated in Haiti.

I have made the personal journey of evolution from obedient Catholic, dutiful daughter, and suburban housewife, to a full-time financial planner and breadwinner. Now I am a catalyst in helping women transform their relationship with money and turn it into an agent of change. Through my work with the Women's Perspective, I am following a call that brings me face-to-face with global economics. I travel to Haiti and Bosnia to participate in projects that are helping to improve the lives of people on a scale that is small but empowering.

The box that contains my life has enlarged well beyond my original imaginings. I am a work-in-progress, continuing to realize the enormity of the spiritual context of our world. As my awareness grows, so does my desire to bring other women into ways of expanding their worlds. I do this with conviction because I know that, in this process, I have arrived at a fuller version of womanhood and personhood. And I do it because I have experienced the peace that comes with living a life expressed through work that matters.

An invitation . . .

I am glad that you have decided to look at two of the most important aspects of your life together: your relationship with money and your relationship with the Divine.
A Woman's Book of Money & Spiritual Vision offers tools to help you explore and examine how you relate to money and how money connects to your faith, your spiritual beliefs, and your relationship to yourself and to your God.

Now that you hold this book in your hands, I invite you to take it seriously and to prepare yourself for your own personal adventure of exploring your beliefs and behaviors. Think about this possibility: Reading this book about money at THIS time in your life may be part of the divine architecture of your life, just as writing it is a part of mine. Once you can begin to accept that the timing is right for you to do this, you can see it as the beginning of important work for you.

By going through the exercises in this book, you can achieve alignment between your financial beliefs and spiritual values. You can take control of your finances so you don't squander, waste, or give up control of your money. And you can do it without sacrificing what you really want to do in life, at the deepest levels of your purpose in life.

I hope this experience will be transformative and freeing for you, one that will open doors in your imagination to new ways of seeing, believing, and doing.

These are the kinds of questions I will be asking you to consider along the way:

❀ Am I a generous person?

❀ How do I give to myself?

❀ How do I give my time, my possessions, my money to others?

❀ How much are my economic transactions influenced by my values? How much are they motivated by habit?

Each time you see this symbol, it is an invitation to record your personal thoughts and responses.

I invite you to use this book as your personal diary, write in it, scribble notes in the margins, capture your ideas and insights. You may also want to start a journal or a notebook in which to keep or record your thoughts. The medium doesn't matter, but the message does. Express your reactions, positive or negative, because both contain valuable insights. There is no formula you must follow other than to record your responses and observations for future reflection.

I recommend that you consider embarking on this spiritual money journey with a group of women... or at least one other woman. While this book can be your guide, other people can be your coaches in this endeavor. By gathering together, you can give each other incentive and encouragement to complete the process and take the next step. If you decide to share your experiences as a group, it will be helpful to establish some basic "ground rules" for your time together, such as agreeing to be open with each other and to hold the information you share in confidentiality.

Of course it is also useful to do this work alone. Your challenge will be to be honest with yourself about the subject of finances and to encourage yourself along the way.

A quick inventory . . .

Before you go further, I am going to ask you to take a few minutes to complete the following quick inventory of what you now understand about your financial life.

1. My financial life is:

___ **in order**

___ **could use some work**

___ **a mess**

___ **a catastrophe**

___ **being taken care of by someone else**

___ **other** _____

My financial life

My financial life

2. My financial facts are:

___ clear to me   ___ unknown

___ readily available   ___ missing

___ confusing

___ other _____

3. When I consider my financial life, I feel:

___ ready to know more   ___ overwhelmed

___ open to some input   ___ confused

___ secure   ___ scared

___ calm   ___ angry

___ embarrassed

4. When I consider my spiritual life:

___ I believe there is a Divinity.

___ I feel very removed from the idea of Divinity.

___ I'm not sure what I believe.

5. I spend time in prayer or meditation:

___ daily

___ frequently

___ once in a while

___ hardly ever

6. I would describe my spiritual life as:

___ Active

___ Dormant

___ More of a "sometimes" thing

___ Unable to describe

What does money mean to you? . . .

Conclude your personal inventory by answering, as directly as you can, this question: What does money mean to me? Jot down what comes immediately to mind, without analyzing or judging your immediate responses.

Money means...

To be poor means...

To be rich means...

My responses

To have enough means...

When I share what I have, I feel...

Read with the intention to change, for every possibility is open to you.

Every possibility . . .

Margaret Wheatley, author of *Leadership and the New Sciences,* tells us, "There is only what we create through our engagement with others and with events. Nothing really transfers; everything is always new and different and unique to each of us. Reality depends upon your engagement."

I hope your engagement with this book brings new insights and a respect for the power of your faith in combination with the power of your resources. Read it with the intention to change, for every possibility is open to you.

Part One

Holy One, Sustainer of all things, give me the courage to look at my financial life with clear sight. Give me the strength to merge the beliefs of my soul with the reality of my money. Give me the knowledge to know what true wealth is and how to use it. When I get distracted, call my attention back. And help me to start by uncovering the messages that have shaped my thinking.

This section will help you . . .

- Uncover the hidden beliefs that motivate your financial life.

- Take the first step to financial freedom.

- Begin to develop the connection between your financial life and your spiritual life.

Chapter One

Your Money Messages

"The Queen was in the parlor . . ."

"The King was in the counting house

counting out his money.

The Queen was in the parlor

eating bread and honey."

As many times as a child that I recited these lines from "Sing a Song of Sixpence," I never imagined that they would pop into my head forty years later at the precise moment they were most applicable.

Yet, there I was, the only woman and newest member of the private banking department of a large commercial bank, sitting at a conference table with seven men in an elegant cherry-paneled board room. The vice-president expounded on the new marketing plan for several minutes before he turned to the group and asked, "Does anyone have a comment?"

A few of the men murmured some compliments, and then I spoke up. I believed I had an important point to make, an enhancement to the plan.

The Money Journey Circle

"To undo our very ancient and very stuck habitual patterns of mind requires that we begin to turn around some of our most basic assumptions."

—Pema Chodron,
WHEN THINGS FALL APART

So I expressed it. My words then hung in the air and echoed in the room. Silence. Dead silence.

It became very clear to me that I was not expected to say anything. My words were simply ignored, and the vice-president went on as if no one had spoken. And all I could think of, as I observed the faces around the table, was that in this bank conference room the "King" was in charge of the money. And the "Queen" was to have no part of it.

Money is never neutral . . .

Money never seems to be neutral. It has an emotional overlay that contains the attitudes of our parents, our friends, our religious institutions, and the culture. The power of what we have been taught can pop up at any moment, in decisions large and small.

These are what I call "money messages." Our money messages create a system of beliefs that become the rudder of our economic lives for good or for ill. Money messages enter into the activities of the present, turning yesterday's ideas into the driving force for today's actions.

My message from the nursery rhyme was, "Keep quiet about money matters because men deal with money and women don't." Sure, I might make a simple suggestion, or ask a question when appropriate, but I normally did not argue for my point of view. Then when I did make a major point in the bank's high-level environment—wham—the message to be quiet hit me directly. (I guess the others in the room had heard the same rhyme, too, or a similar one. No one acted in a way that showed they believed I had the right to speak or be acknowledged!)

My messages about money contain the attitudes of my mother, my grandmother, and other family members from both sides. But that's not all. They also contain the history of my life, the information I've absorbed from home, school, church, movies, music, magazines, and friendships. And so do yours.

Perhaps if I share more of my life story with you, I can illustrate what I mean. I am a white, North American woman who grew up as the only child of a widow in the Northeast in a middle-class family. I was raised Catholic and influenced by the Jewish family of my deceased father. I went to a Catholic high school and college.

> *Money messages contain the attitudes of your mother, your grandmother, your family . . . information from school, church, movies, music, magazines, and friendships.*

As a college student, and later a wife married to a young corporate executive, living in suburban Connecticut and raising five children, I was locked into a set of beliefs and attitudes that kept my world in a very small box. The outlines of that box were drawn by color, genes, geographic location, class, religion, education, marriage, along with many other more minor details.

After my divorce, my life changed, and so did the outline of my box. I was now a single parent who cared for my children while I worked as a banker, financial planner, and consultant to nonprofit organizations. I interacted daily with people and their money. In this role I gained new perspective. As I observed others making financial decisions, I noticed that they—and I—always wanted more of everything, and most of us were never satisfied. The annual raise or the bonus always brought with it new desires and needs.

As I began to work with my own new awareness and to question others about their money motives, I found we shared many similarities. I also began to notice behaviors that did not seem connected to the current circumstances in a person's life. I began to recognize that "money messages" always make an appearance—with an intensely personal agenda.

Money myths always show up . . .

Sometimes money messages come to light in surprising moments. I was visiting a friend of mine, a successful attorney, and she was talking about a favorite topic of mine—money messages. She was disagreeing with me about the role of unconscious agendas: "I don't think I fall prey to any of that. I am so analytical. I think everything through, and go over and over the details until I come to a clear decision."

We happened to be sitting in her living room, which was filled with books and bookshelves. In fact, she had so many books, she had added extra shelves in the dining room and over the door jams. As she sat back to think about what she had just said, she glanced around the room and started smiling. The smile spread across her whole face, and she laughed out loud.

"Okay, okay," she said. "I see what you mean. I am analytical about everything except books. And do you want to know why? When I was a young girl, my father would give me an allowance and say, 'Spend your money wisely. Do not be frivolous and buy things you don't need. But books, books are not frivolous. Always surround yourself with good books.' And look at what I've done, without even realizing it. I am surrounded by good books!"

Money messages are different for each of us, though many of us have heard similar ones, bound as we are by our generation and our ethnic or geographic origins. Usually the money story we live by is inherited. It may be generations old—and the strength of our ties to this history may bind us in ways that are not apparent to our conscious mind—but the story we learn keeps unfolding over time. What we are taught will show up in some way!

In my household, as in many others, when I was growing up, money was a private affair. It was a family matter, never to be discussed outside the house—and, sometimes, not even inside it! Girls, especially, were often told not to ask questions about how much things cost or not to "worry your pretty head about that." As if "that" were a taboo subject.

In a workshop I was presenting on the subject of money messages, long about mid-afternoon one participant, a nun who was the manager of special project funds for her Order, stood up and said, "Stop! I just had a flashback. I saw my mother putting my father's weekly salary in envelopes labeled for all our expenses."

She then went on to say, "Do you know I have set up the accounts in the same way for the Motherhouse? Now I understand why I have such a difficult time saying 'yes' to anyone who comes to me for funds for a new project. It is simply not on the books. There is not a category for it! No envelope! My mother would say no to new things because the money was always already distributed in the envelopes. It was all accounted for beforehand. There was no room for creativity or discussion."

Originally money was designed to be an economic tool, but in our society it has come to represent much more than just a way to exchange goods and services. The question I put to you is this: How aware are you of the emotional overtones of your money—whether it is earned, inherited, won, given as allowance, received as a gift or in the settlement of a dispute?

The first stage of your money journey . . .

The diagram on the facing page is a picture of the six stages of The Money Journey Circle that you will be working with in this book. The first stage is MONEY MESSAGES: uncovering the messages that have been implanted into your unconsciousness—often without your even knowing it. This is the stage of awareness, of understanding the money mythology you have believed in and have lived out.

It is critically important to know what the messages behind your financial actions are, but these subtle "rules" you live by may be hard to uncover because they are so deeply embedded. That is why I suggest that you write down your thoughts and responses as we take this money journey together. This will give you a chance to step back and examine how these themes affect your current life and gain more understanding of the power these messages have on your behavior.

The process starts with exploring how you learned about money. I believe that nothing in life, including the messages you heard in nursery rhymes or parental admonitions, is inconsequential, extraneous, or wasted. The exercises in this chapter will help you uncover those money messages and use that information as the starting point not only to get a grip on your finances but to go forward, and inward, to the spiritual connection to money.

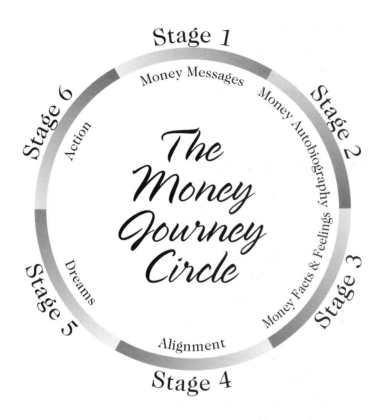

Stage 1, MONEY MESSAGES:
The myths about money you grew up with, believe in and live out.

Stage 2, MONEY AUTOBIOGRAPHY:
The story of your experiences and relationships with money.

Stage 3, MONEY FACTS & FEELINGS:
The uncovering of your financial facts and how you feel about them.

Stage 4, ALIGNMENT:
The integration of your facts, feelings, and actions with your spiritual core.

Stage 5, DREAMS:
The exploration of your call.

Stage 6, ACTION:
The formation of your future through specific steps.

You will be asked to remember, imagine, write, examine, evaluate, listen to other's stories, and acknowledge JUST WHAT IS THE STORY YOU LEARNED ABOUT MONEY. It will then be up to you to decide if you want to keep your myth or develop a new story that is compatible with the way you want to live your life now.

For me, when I recognized one of my myths, I realized I no longer wanted to be the "Queen" who was not allowed to think, speak, or deal with money. I replaced it with a new story, one that I will share with you throughout this book. And one that is evolving yet.

Now, it is time to explore your own money messages, myths, and stories.

Family patterns . . .

The process of uncovering money messages takes time. Remember, you are developing a composite view of yourself and of your belief system.

This first set of questions will help you identify the family money patterns you experienced as you were growing up. Again and again, in workshops and individual discussions, I have seen revelations emerge as women have answered the eight questions that follow. Answer each question as directly as you can, remembering that there is no right or wrong answer. There is only an awareness of your thinking patterns, your attitudes, and your motivations.

1. When you were growing up, who handled the money in your family? Who made the major financial decisions?

2. How were money decisions or problems handled? Was money discussed openly ? Who was a part of the discussion?

3. Describe how you saw a major financial decision being made.

My family patterns

My family patterns

4. Did you think that the money available in your household was scarce or abundant? What did you hear or see that created this perception?

5. When you look back, do you think your perception of the money supply at home was accurate? Was your perception the result of your own observation or based on what someone else told you?

6. Do you remember how you actually felt about money as a child? Write a sentence or two describing your feelings.

7. Describe a childhood experience related to money that has stayed in your mind.

8. What feelings surface for you when you think of the money history of your family?

My family patterns

Money doesn't grow on trees . . .

Pennies from heaven . . .

Don't talk about the family finances outside this house . . .

You can never be too rich or too thin . . .

Waste not, want not . . .

Don't be ashamed of being poor . . .

God loves a cheerful giver . . .

It's only money . . .

We can't afford that . . .

A penny saved is a penny earned . . .

When I win big . . .

When my ship comes in . . .

Be grateful for what you have . . .

Appearances are everything . . .

Check the day-old counter . . .

A fool and his money are soon parted . . .

NEVER SPEND THE PRINCIPAL . . .

Make do . . .

We're poor, but we're happy . . .

Always save for a rainy day . . .

Time your shopping to coincide with the sales . . .

Buy low, sell high . . .

Shop till you drop . . .

Don't worry about that . . .

Time is money . . .

Money is the root of all evil . . .

THERE IS PLENTY OF MONEY . . .

You can have it all! . . .

Money can't buy happiness . . .

It's greedy to want more . . .

Catchy phrases . . .

Money messages come in many forms, some obvious, some covert. You may have heard catchy phrases, such as those the facing page, that stick in your mind. Or you may have been given nonverbal messages, which may take longer to identify but are just as powerful.

Money messages come from many sources, not just from people you know but also from the culture: books, movies, art, plays, music, advertising or political slogans and other oft-used phrases.

Take a few minutes now to respond to the following six questions about money messages that have influenced your life. For each, write down as many messages as you can remember. Don't ponder each one too long; just start to write. One message will trigger the next until you come to a resting spot. If you cannot remember any messages, note that and go on. More messages may rise up in your consciousness as the days go by. Just keep adding them to your list.

Jotting down these words may sound silly or simple at first, but repeated phrases and other ingrained expectations can have a viselike grip on the mind, and this is a great way to understand their hold.

1. What messages about money did your mother give you?

My money messages

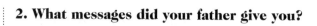

My money messages

2. What messages did your father give you?

3. Your grandparents?

4. Your friends?

5. Your religious training?

6. Your teachers?

Putting things into context . . .

Understanding not only your family role models, but how the family models affect your current financial life, is the cornerstone of putting your financial values into spiritual perspective. It is important to keep writing down your responses. The act of writing what you are aware of will keep the process in motion.

These next six questions focus on where you are today, financially and spiritually.

1. Who handles the money in your present life? Who makes the major financial decisions?

2. How are money decisions or problems handled in your home today? Is money discussed openly? Who is a part of the discussion?

My family patterns

3. Describe how major financial decisions are made in your present household?

4. Is the money available in your household scarce or abundant?

5. What feelings surface for you as you think of your current money scene?

6. What similarities do you see between your past and your present attitudes or behavior around money?

Decisions, decisions . . .

"Climb up my apple tree

Slide down my cellar door

And we'll be jolly friends forever more."

My mother always used to sing this little song to me. Many years later when I was married and had a family, my husband and I were searching for a new house. One of the listings we saw had both an apple tree and a cellar door. I loved it and we bought it. I was so happy to be in the house that I had often imagined from my mother's song. What made me even happier was that I could pass on the joy of "an apple tree and a cellar door" to my kids.

A few years later, it was time to move again. Our next purchase was a large English Tudor-style house. After we bought it, I happened to be looking through my husband's old family pictures And there it was—the old English Tudor that had belonged to his grandmother and where he had spent a lot of time in his childhood. It looked exactly the same as our new home.

These two examples showed me clearly that even the biggest economic decision, such as buying a house, is influenced by messages from childhood that have little to do with current financial calculations.

In fact, money messages seem to surface most often when we have a big decision to make. They may come to the forefront as admonitions, background, warnings, or criticism. Sometimes the message itself is unclear, but we have an uneasy feeling or a sense of doubt that keeps us from deciding.

Money message seem to surface most often when you have a big decision to make.

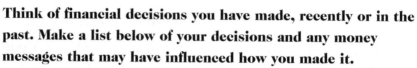

**Think of financial decisions you have made, recently or in the
past. Make a list below of your decisions and any money
messages that may have influenced how you made it.**

My decisions

DECISION	MONEY MESSAGE

What matters to you? . . .

By uncovering money messages, you are getting to your core attitudes and values—the very roots of your belief system. This process brings you face-to-face with some fundamental questions: Do you want to keep the myth you have developed beginning in childhood? Or do you want to create a message that is more compatible with your life now?

Early messages have a lot of power. It is hard to question the system you were raised in, or to disagree with it. Even if you question the beliefs only in your own mind, you will feel the power of the pattern.

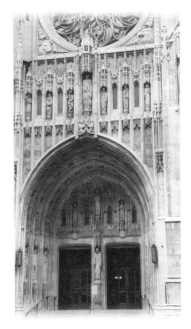

Breaking the rules or stepping outside the code of behavior embedded in the system in which you were raised can be paralyzing. Often, keeping the rules is the only way to remain a part of the tribe, family, community, or religion. Break the rules, and you're out.

I witnessed this first-hand as a child. My mother, an Irish Catholic, married a German Jewish man. She defied the systems—ethnic, religious, and family—and was held accountable. She could no longer participate in the rituals of her own church because she had defied its rule not to marry outside the faith. Exclusion is a powerful lesson.

As an inquiring woman, you are questioning and coming to terms with your history, your financial life, and your spiritual life. In some cases, that may mean changing a particular message, or removing it from your mind.

Remember my friend with all the books? Even as she

laughed about being surrounded by books, acknowledging the situation allowed her to evaluate the money message she had inherited: that books could be her only luxury. Once she became aware of the power of her father's message, she was able to move beyond his rules about what she could buy for enjoyment.

In my case, the change was not so lighthearted. The severity of my financial situation required me to make major changes, and quickly. I was a divorced mother of five children without any support other than my salary. I also carried with me a deeply imbedded message: "Do not talk about your finances outside the household."

That had to change. It was a survival issue. At the doctor's office, the orthodontist, the lawyer's office, the financial aid offices of the colleges my children attended—at all these places I had to loudly, clearly, and truthfully talk about the reality of my finances.

I was being pushed and prodded, for the sake of providing for myself and my children, to see the message of silence about money as untrue and useless for my present time and place. My mother's admonition to keep money matters a "family matter" acted as bondage, holding me to the myth. It was time for a new message.

Change is what can happen when you hold your money messages up to the light. But not every money message must go. Your task is to listen to each message that you have identified, understand its history, and evaluate the current use of that message. Do you want to keep it? Use it? Change it? Get rid of it? These next three questions will help you consider what messages still have value for you and what money messages no longer work.

1. Which money messages that you grew up with are still true for you today? How do they influence you?

MESSAGE	INFLUENCE

My money messages

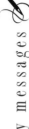

My money messages

2. Which money messages are not helpful to you now? Why?

UNHELPFUL MESSAGE	WHY?

3. Which money messages have value for you now? What is that value?

VALUABLE MESSAGE   VALUE

My money messages

Recap . . .

In the work you've done in this first chapter, I hope some new insights have come to you about the influences your MONEY MESSAGES have on your current attitudes toward money. Understanding these habitual ways of thinking can open the windows of your mind to new understandings and possible beliefs.

With this awareness comes the opportunity to develop a new money mythology based on your own values, an opportunity to develop your personal response to your financial life. This is the true meaning of financial "response-ability."

As you continue on your money journey, I invite you to thoughtfully and prayerfully exercise your ability to respond to your own situation—truthfully, creatively, and purposefully.

Chapter Two

Your Money Autobiography

What is your history? . . .

Researchers are beginning to find that our bodies carry our emotional history in cellular memory as well as in mental memory. The ideas we hold become the operating system under which we live, move, and have our being. I believe this system of ideas has a presence as strong as our DNA, but instead of genetic material, it is made up of our family philosophy, cultural ethos, and spiritual beliefs.

It is only when we "unpack" our emotional history that we can become aware of any patterned responses, motivating ideas, and habitual behavior. That is why I believe the second stage of The Money Journey Circle, writing your MONEY AUTOBIOGRAPHY, is so important. Telling the story of your experiences and relationships with money has the potential to reveal many secrets about how you have related—and are still relating— to money in your life.

The
Money
Journey
Circle

"Learning to think objectively about money is the key to making yourself free."

— Eliot Janeway,
contemporary economist

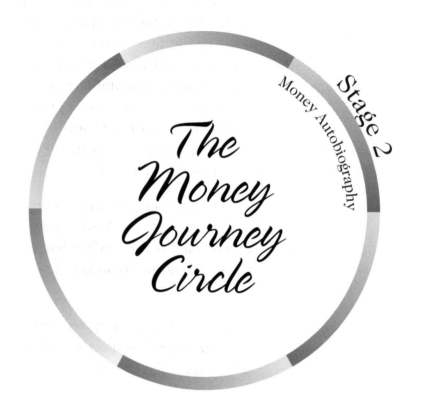

The Money Journey Circle

Money Autobiography

Stage 2

You will need to set aside time to write your money autobiography. Some people resist this, or find it hard to begin. However, there is a freedom that comes from writing a money autobiography that makes it well worth your time and effort.

Since money messages are not always apparent to the conscious mind, sometimes they will unfold only by questioning or in conversation. You may find it helpful to prepare your money autobiography with a group, or at least one other person, since your story or myth was developed in a group. Having a group to work with may help you examine your story more honestly. In solitude we are more prone to rationalize, deny, embellish, or otherwise distort the truth. The sharing of our stories, questions, and insights can be very important in helping us see an emerging pattern.

This said, it is still valuable to do this work even if you don't have a group to work with. You can speak out loud to yourself. And you can challenge yourself: "Is this really what happened? Have I conveniently 'forgotten' some key elements?"

However you approach it, this process of writing your own story will provide you with the historical perspective of how your current relationship with money developed.

Starting your money autobiography . . .

The next few pages present a series of money autobiography questions that will help you recall your experiences and remember the feelings associated with each event. The questions are designed to help you think about any and all of the conditions that influenced your perception of the world and of the role of money in your life.

Take each of the questions one at a time and write, in narrative form, the scenes, experiences, and feelings that come to mind. Remember, this is your money story. There is no right or wrong way to do this; simply note the experiences and feelings that come to mind.

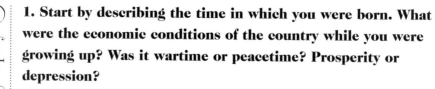

My money autobiography

1. Start by describing the time in which you were born. What were the economic conditions of the country while you were growing up? Was it wartime or peacetime? Prosperity or depression?

2. Next, describe your family configuration. Two parents? A single parent? Adoptive parents? Foster parents? Other siblings? Presence of grandparents?

My money autobiography

My money autobiography

3. Describe your first home as best you can remember, noting how early the memory is. Did you live in a house or apartment? Was it large, small? In a town, city or farm, another country? Did you have your own room, or did you share a room? How did this change over the years?

4. What are your early memories of family holidays? Vacations? Shopping Trips?

My money autobiography

My money autobiography

5. Make note of any role models you had, real or fictional. What did they represent to you?

6. What are your memories of high school? Of clothes, cars, friends, parties, dates, sports, grades? What were the fashions, books, movies, ads, or trends of this time?

My money autobiography

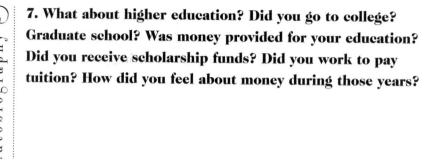

7. What about higher education? Did you go to college? Graduate school? Was money provided for your education? Did you receive scholarship funds? Did you work to pay tuition? How did you feel about money during those years?

8. Describe your first job and how much you earned. What was your experience of opening your first bank account, making your first investment, buying your first car, renting your first apartment, buying your first house, etc.?

My money autobiography

9. Move on to describe advancing in your career, growing your business, marrying, starting a family, raising children, etc.

10. Talk about making contributions to religious institutions and giving to social and charitable causes.

My money autobiography

11. What are your memories of religious experiences in your community—sacraments, bar mitzvahs, celebrations, revivals, funerals? Make note of any special words you remember being said to you.

12. How has your gender affected your relationship with money?

My money autobiography

My money autobiography

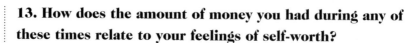

13. How does the amount of money you had during any of these times relate to your feelings of self-worth?

Creating a money history timeline . . .

By answering these questions about your experience of money as you were growing up, you have captured on paper an image of the circumstances of the life you were born into, and the information you assimilated. At the time you were living it, you did not have the advantage of perspective. You simply absorbed what was happening.

Given the amount of data you have already remembered, you may be beginning to get a clearer picture of your money myths and how they fit with your personal economic situation—and that of the larger world at that particular time. I want you to take this one step further and plot your responses into a money history timeline. This is a valuable tool that can help you break a lot of information down into manageable chunks.

On the timeline on the following pages, write in the years for each decade of your life. (If you feel you would like more space to write, simply use a blank sheet of paper or your journal.) Review each of the money autobiography questions you have already answered and jot a few words of summary in the appropriate decades. Above the line, write your more pleasant or satisfying experiences. Below the line, write your more unpleasant or unsatisfying experiences.

For example, during your high school years, you might write above the line:

Baby-sitting jobs - first personal spending money!

Below the line, you might write:

Clothes - parents always angry about costs.

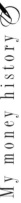

My money history

MONEY HISTORY TIME LINE

Pleasant, satisfying experiences

Year	19___	19___	19___
Age	0	10	20

Unpleasant, unsatisfying experiences

MONEY HISTORY TIME LINE

Pleasant, satisfying experiences

My money history

Year ___   ___   ___
Age 30   40   50

Unpleasant, unsatisfying experiences

My money history

MONEY HISTORY TIME LINE

Pleasant, satisfying experiences

Year ___   ___   ___   ___

Age 60   70   80   90

Unpleasant, unsatisfying experiences

Sacred space . . .

One of my favorite recommendations to women, at this stage of the journey, is to give yourself some sacred space. By that, I mean interior space, a place where you can rest and accept the person that you are and the gifts you have been given.

Think for a moment about how you might create this space for yourself. Prayer and meditation are a few of the ways to access your sacred space. I often promise myself I will take time to be quiet, regularly. I will start by making sure I have a specific time to meditate every day. I determine to put the thoughts of what I have to do, and when and why, out of my head as best as I can. But then, after a while, I stop the practice. I find it hard to continue this type of disciplined commitment to quiet time. Sound familiar?

Do not be discouraged, and do not give up. If one way of creating a sacred space does not work out for you, another one will. Determine to sequester yourself at planned intervals. It will benefit you and all those who know you.

A friend creates her sacred space by putting on soft music—flute or harp—as soon as she wakes up. She lights a candle in her bedroom to remind her of the light of the divine. Then she goes about getting dressed.

I find this works for me, too. When I set the stage and purposefully move into that space, holding it sacred, even in the busiest times of day I can move back into my quiet space. When I do not do this—when I am too busy, too distracted to set up my space—I lose my grounding for making adjustments to the reality of the day.

However you create sacred space for yourself, it will help you develop resiliency. Having this quiet place in your home—and in your mind—creates a place where you can bring the surprises that have the potential to throw you off kilter. Don't struggle to make your space mimic someone else's idea. Make it your own, whatever that looks or feels like for you.

My sacred space

Write a promise to yourself to create a sacred space. Be specific about how, when, and where you will set aside your space.

Recap . . .

Congratulations! Your first two stages of the Money Journey are nearly complete: your search for your MONEY MESSAGES and your MONEY AUTOBIOGRAPHY. It is time to go back to the words of Eliot Janeway from the opening of this chapter:

> *"Learning to think objectively about money*
> *is the key to making yourself free."*

This is the message I hope you are beginning to experience. The work you are doing now is about freedom—the freedom to make decisions about what you really want without being restrained by ignorance, by other people's beliefs, or by the temptation to yield control over the money in your life.

There are many tracks that lead to bringing your financial life into spiritual perspective. And there will be moments on this journey when the process may seem like two steps forward and one step back. But be assured: *You have made the most difficult decision of all—the decision to begin.*

Ending prayer . . .

In my reading of the twentieth-century theologian Teilhard de Chardin, author of the *Divine Milieu,* I am inspired to think of the two threads of our lives: an inner thread and an outer thread. The inner thread contains all the ideas, attitudes, and learnings of our life to date. The outer thread is composed of the circumstances we find ourselves in at any given moment. Use this prayer as you continue to seek understanding and perspective on the role of money in your life:

> *Guide me to have the persistence to find my inner and outer threads. Help me to have the courage to hold these threads up to the light, so that I can see the whole tapestry that is me, in body and soul. Lead me to see both the strengths and weaknesses of the weavings of my life. May I have the love to bind the threads together, so that doubled, they may work doubly hard for my good and the good of the world.*
>
> *—My interpretation of Teilhard de Chardin*

Resources . . .

Divine Milieu, Teilhard de Chardin (New York: HarperCollins, 1989).
> Explains how we can enter into cooperative activity with God, making our spiritual life part of the continuing evolution of the universe.

Anatomy of the Spirit: The Seven Stages of Power and Healing, Carolyn Myss (New York: Random House, 1997).
> A good description of the relationship between the physical, energetic, and spiritual systems of a human being.

Cry Pain, Cry Hope: Thresholds to Purpose, Elizabeth O'Connor (Washington D.C., Potter's House, 1993).
> A guide to the dimensions of call.

Our Many Selves, Elizabeth O'Connor (this book is out of print but worth it if you can find it).
> A handbook to self-discovery.

Molecules of Emotion: Why You Feel the Way You Feel, Candace B. Pert (New York: Simon & Schuster, 1999).
> This book offers excellent information on cellular memory.

Leadership and the New Science: Discovering Order in a Chaotic World, Margaret J. Wheatley (San Francisco: Berrett-Koehler, 1999).
> This book offers an understanding of chaos as a necessary part of organization and growth.

Part Two

Chapter 3: Uncovering Your Money Facts & Feelings

Chapter 4: Creating Alignment

Creator, Friend, guide my hands, my head, and my heart to the facts and figures of my financial life. Open my spirit to the transformation and freedom that the knowledge of those details can bring. Prepare my soul for using money wisely in ways that can truly enrich me and those around me in the world, near and far.

This section will help you . . .

❀ "De-fuzz" your thinking about your financial numbers.

❀ Go straight to the financial facts of your life.

❀ Identify your feelings about what money you have
and what money you owe.

❀ Answer some key questions: How much do I really need?
What are my choices for spending? What do I want to use
my money for?

❀ Begin to align the reality of your financial situation
with your core beliefs.

Chapter Three

Uncovering Your Money Facts & Feelings

Count your blessings . . .

In this chapter I will be asking you to identify specifics about your financial resources. But before you start to "count the money," I want you to "count your blessings." That might include your health, your intellectual capacity, family, friends, spiritual connections, community, even the small "riches" you have—such as the unique clock you picked up in a European flea market when you were a college student traveling on five dollars a day; the series of photos of your family and friends; a pair of ratty old slippers that soothe your tired feet at the end of the day better than any fancy shoes.

Take note, too, of the intangible riches: the knowledge that your best friend would be at your side in a minute if you called; that your community would help you in any emergency; that you can trust yourself and your intuition to take you to the next best step for yourself.

The
Money
Journey
Circle

"The challenge of mindfulness is to work with the very circumstances that you find yourself in."
—Jon Kabat Zin,
FULL CATASTROPHE LIVING

Does your real abundance come from a close friend you trust? A partner who listens to you? Children who are bringing your good counsel to reality in the daily story of their lives? Think, too, of important lessons—even good things—that have come out of difficult challenges you have faced, and of their value to you at this time in your life.

In places like the United States where money has such a high priority, we can easily lose sight of its place. Money is not the soul of existence, and we need to put our financial lives in perspective. This is not to deny the reality that money has its uses. One thought that comes to my mind when I do this next exercise is a shopping trip with an African friend. She spent her bonus on family and friends. At first, I was concerned that she was spending so much. Then she put my thoughts to rest.

"Money is nothing," she said. "Life is all about relationships. It makes me happy to buy these gifts, and everyone will be happy that I remembered them." At the top of my lists of abundances I, too, put my connections to other people. What is at the top of your list?

Describe the wealth and abundance in your life that does not have a dollar sign attached to it.

My blessings

My blessings

What do you know? . . .

Many of us simply do not know the facts of our financial life. We might even prefer it that way. Or, in the words of a woman who participated in one of my workshops, "I like to keep my numbers fuzzy because then I do not have to take responsibility for them."

In my own life, there were many times when I could not bring myself to look directly at the facts of my financial life. Or I would look at some things, but not others. One of my favorite approaches to money issues was to play Scarlet, the heroine of "Gone With the Wind," and repeat after her: "I'll worry about that tomorrow."

For many years I would not look at my financial picture . . . I knew that once I understood the situation, I would have to make some decisions.

I would find myself picking and choosing facts. I'd rationalize away anything that I didn't know or couldn't take care of. I'd tell myself that I was being responsible just because I took care of one easy thing, like paying a bill, and left the rest undone.

For many years, I would not look at the whole picture all at once. It was just too big for me. And I knew that once I understood the situation, I would have to make some decisions. I would have to accept the responsibility of becoming the primary decision maker in my family's financial affairs.

Now, I realize I was afraid of making decisions because I was afraid I would do the wrong thing. The second realization was that I did not have enough information to make an informed decision.

On the pages that follow, I am going to ask you to take an

honest look at your financial facts… and then move beyond the details of those facts, to know the details but not get stuck on them. This "Facts & Feelings" stage of The Money Journey Circle starts with some fundamental questions, such as, "Do you know where your financial records are maintained? If you can't find something, do you know where you can look? If you have questions, do you know someone you could call for help?"

But uncovering the necessary data is only half the picture. The important parallel is to discover and connect with your emotional response to these facts. If you will take this section slowly, one segment at a time, I can help you do that.

Financial awareness checklist . . .

I am going to start you on your exploration with the following Financial Awareness Checklist. The goal is to help you identify what you know ... and where you need to find out more. This is not the time to worry or feel guilty; this is information for your awareness only.

My financial awareness

DO YOU ...	YES	NO
Have a checking account or credit cards in your own name? (For example, if you are married, is it under Jane Doe, not Mrs. John Doe?)	___	___
Have a banker?	___	___
Know your banker?	___	___
Have a broker?	___	___
Know your broker?	___	___
Have an attorney?	___	___
Know your attorney?	___	___
Have an accountant?	___	___
Know your accountant?	___	___
Know if you could borrow money in your own name?	___	___

DO YOU . . .	YES	NO
Know what your credit report prepared by the major credit bureaus looks like?	____	____
Know how to get a credit report sent to you?	____	____
Make your own investment decisions?	____	____
Understand the tax return you sign?	____	____
Understand your retirement benefits?	____	____
Understand your spouse's retirement benefits and what are your rights to collect on them?	____	____
Have an Individual Retirement Account (IRA)?	____	____
Know your current insurance needs?	____	____
Know the specifics of your insurance coverage:		
Property?	____	____
Auto?	____	____
Health?	____	____
Disability?	____	____
Have a current Will?	____	____

My financial awareness

My financial awareness

PUT A CHECK next to any of the following that you own in your own name:

__Real Estate

__Mutual Funds

__Treasury Bills

__Car

__Stocks

__CDs

__Valuable personal property

__Bonds

__Savings Bonds

PUT A CHECK next to any of the following terms that you could explain easily to a friend:

__Net Worth

__Stock

__IRA

__Cash Flow

__Bond

__Annuity

__Treasury Bills

__Mutual Fund

__CD

__Stock Options

__Prime Rate

__Compound Interest

DO YOU regularly do any of the following:	YES	NO
Read financial books, magazines, or the financial section of your local or a national newspaper?	___	___
Listen to the financial news on television?	___	___
Visit web sites that contain financial information and instruction?	___	___

Take a deep breath . . . you may have just crossed over into new territory, but you don't have to travel the entire country all at once. Remember: This is a time for awareness, not for pressure or guilt or fear. You can take the time you need. For now, take just a few more minutes to respond to these two reflective questions:

What gaps in your financial information do you want to fill in?

My financial awareness

How are you feeling right now as you start to get clearer about the breadth and depth of your understanding of basic financial facts?

Getting over the hurdles . . .

As I was in the middle of writing this chapter, I received the following e-mail from Candice Briggs of Battle Creek, Michigan, and I want to share it with you:

As a self-employed counselor for over twenty-five years I am most interested in the emotional blocks that we place upon ourselves in relationship to money. As a Christian, I learned at a young age that "the love of money is wrong," and I have somehow twisted that to not allowing myself to experience money exchanges in a healthy way. Many women my age, in our fifties, turn to our spouses, who may not know the answers either, so we sit and "hope" and wait for something to rescue us from the "unknown" world of finance. It is my desire to understand finances more clearly and become more confident in my choices both spiritually and financially. It is time for me to face the fears that I have created around money and move ahead to help others.

Perhaps one of the biggest hurdles to get over in understanding your finances more clearly is to find all of your data. Many women are tempted to stop here because they simply don't know where things are.

One woman I know used to put important papers on top of the refrigerator. The problem was, she forgot what she put there and some of them fell to the floor behind the refrigerator. It wasn't until she moved from the house that she found those important papers. Note: Be wary of certain nontraditional storage places!

Become a collector . . .

Being organized is a part of money management. There are several good books listed at the end of this chapter on how to get organized, and what blocks you from creating and maintaining order. For the moment, however, I want you to simply get a container that appeals to you—a cardboard box, a plastic storage unit, an unused suitcase—or clear out a drawer. This container will become the temporary repository for your financial paperwork. You can organize your papers in a different form later, if you choose, but for now, just having the data collected in one place will be a strong aide to moving forward.

Take your time. Even as you look for your records, you can continue to work on your money issues. You may be the kind of person who wants to spend three hours tracking down everything. Or you may prefer to take fifteen minutes a day until it is all done.

Remember to be attentive and prayerful as you gather information. Inspiration and insights are close at hand. Think of order not as a chore, but as a quality of spirit.

Here is a list of the records you will need to collect. As you find each one and put it in your special container, check it off on the list. Remind yourself that this space is holding the tools you need to move forward on your spiritual money journey.

Financial document checklist . . .

My financial documents

___ checkbook

___ savings account book

___ bank statements
    ___ checking account
    ___ savings account
    ___ CD account
    ___ money market account

___ payroll stubs for one month

___ insurance policies
    ___ life insurance
    ___ health insurance
    ___ disability insurance
    ___ homeowner's or renter's insurance
    ___ auto insurance

___ brokerage statements
    ___ bonds
    ___ stocks
    ___ mutual funds
    ___ annuities

___ car title

___ property deeds

___ list of contents of your safe deposit box

___ safe deposit keys

___ records of all retirement funds

___ copy of your will

___ copy of Power of Attorney

___ copy of Health Proxy

___ deed to cemetery plot

___ loan statements
    ___ home mortgage loan balance
    ___ auto loan balance
    ___ student loan balance
    ___ other loan balances

___ most recent credit card statements

_____

_____

_____

_____

_____

___ copy of your credit history

My financial documents

In the dark no more . . .

If there is no pressing, specific reason for looking at financial details, most people—women AND men—do not have financial information readily available. Women in particular "are not socialized and educated to take control of their financial destiny," as Beth Ryerson, President of Wells College, has observed.

The good news is that women have the tools to connect to their financial lives. If you have been up in the air about at least some of your financial matters until now, collecting your key financial records will help you get grounded. A good place to start is to record the important names, addresses, phone numbers, account numbers, etc. relating to your finances. This information will not only save you time when you need to know it, but more importantly, will remind you that, though you may have assistance, you are in charge. Knowing the very basic issues, such as where you stash your bank statements or savings account records, will help you grow in your understanding of how you treat your financial life. And it is only as you understand your finances that you will be able to bring them into alignment with your spiritual values.

The next few pages provide some space for you to record the names and contact information for key financial people and institutions in your life. You can use this book as your recordkeeper, or simply use these pages as a model for your own recordkeeping where it is convenient for you, such as on a computer or in a notebook.

1. KEY PEOPLE

ATTORNEY

Name _____

Address _____

Phone _____Fax _____

E-mail_____Website _____

ACCOUNTANT

Name _____

Address _____

Phone _____Fax _____

E-mail_____Website _____

BANKER

Name _____

Address _____

Phone _____Fax _____

E-mail_____Website _____

My resources

My resources

BROKER

Name _____

Address _____

Phone _____ Fax _____

E-mail _____ Website _____

FINANCIAL PLANNER

Name _____

Address _____

Phone _____ Fax _____

E-mail _____ Website _____

INSURANCE AGENT

Name _____

Address _____

Phone _____ Fax _____

E-mail _____ Website _____

PERSON HOLDING POWER OF ATTORNEY

Name _____

Address _____

Phone _____Fax _____

E-mail _____

PERSON HOLDING HEALTH CARE PROXY

Name _____

Address _____

Phone _____Fax _____

E-mail _____

TAX PREPARER

Name _____

Address _____

Phone _____Fax _____

E-mail_____Website _____

My resources

2. BANK, BROKERAGE, MUTUAL FUND, IRA ACCOUNTS

BANK ACCOUNT: CHECKING 1

Institution _____

Account # _____

Address _____

Phone _____ Fax _____

E-mail_____ Website _____

BANK ACCOUNT: CHECKING 2

Institution _____

Account # _____

Address _____

Phone _____ Fax _____

E-mail_____ Website _____

BANK ACCOUNT: SAVINGS

Institution _____

Account # _____

Address _____

Phone _____ Fax _____

E-mail_____ Website _____

BROKERAGE ACCOUNT

Institution _____

Account # _____

Address _____

Phone _____Fax _____

E-mail_____Website _____

MUTUAL FUNDS ACCOUNT

Institution _____

Account # _____

Address _____

Phone _____Fax _____

E-mail_____Website _____

IRA ACCOUNT

Institution _____

Account # _____

Address _____

Phone _____Fax _____

E-mail_____Website _____

My resources

My resources

3. INSURANCE POLICIES

LIFE

Company _____

Phone _____ Fax _____

Type _____ Amount _____

Insured _____

Policy# _____

Policy Owner _____

Beneficiary _____

HEALTH AND HOSPITALIZATION

Company _____

Phone _____ Fax _____

Type _____ Amount _____

Policy# _____

Insured _____

DISABILITY

Company _____

Phone _____ Fax _____

Type _____ Amount _____

Policy# _____

Insured _____

AUTOMOBILE

Company _____

Phone _____ Fax _____

Type _____ Amount _____

Policy# _____

Insured _____

HOMEOWNER'S/RENTER'S

Company _____

Phone _____ Fax _____

Type _____ Amount _____

Policy# _____

Insured _____

My resources

My resources

LIABILITY

Company _____

Phone _____ Fax _____

Type _____ Amount _____

Policy# _____

Insured _____

OTHER

Company _____

Phone _____ Fax _____

Type _____ Amount _____

Policy# _____

Insured _____

OTHER

Company _____

Phone _____ Fax _____

Type _____ Amount _____

Policy# _____

Insured _____

Add other important accounts, names, and numbers that you want to include.

My resources

Take heart . . .

This is the point where some women become overwhelmed just looking at the information that is needed. I like to think of the process of collecting financial data as similar to collecting antiques. When you first find an antique chair, for instance, you need to assess how much it's worth, take a look at any damage that has occurred over time, and then begin the loving work of restoring the chair to usefulness.

If you are uncovering the details of your financial facts for the first time, please be patient with yourself. Move through this chapter slowly. Take heart from the following story of Jan Luckingham Fable, who tells in her own words how she changed her approach to money:

My family of origin was not a wealthy one, but when I was twelve years old, I learned I could sign my name on a store receipt and charge things at a department store. My father thought this was cute. He told me with a smile that I reminded him of his mother. He told me stories about how his mother would impulsively buy a dress or a hat and charge it. And then, later, when my grandfather had a fit about the bill, how she'd deny having bought anything— telling him the store had made a mistake. Next day she'd return the offending item and tell my grandfather the store had corrected the error. The message to me was clear. My paternal grandmother was impulsive and irresponsible about money, and so was I—but it was okay because it made my father smile.

I continued to be impulsive and irresponsible with money for many, many years. I never reconciled a bank statement—in fact, I didn't even open them—until I was well into my forties. And until fairly recently, I continued to rely, without questions, on others, "on the experts," to invest for me, despite the fact that not asking questions in the past had led to a very large loss of money for me.

It's been a long journey from the piles of unopened bank statements and the joy of charging whenever and whatever I wanted. Now, I am self-employed, a homeowner, and diligent about paying credit card balances each month and saving for big purchases and needed home improvements. I've also begun to take an active interest in retirement investing, and I now ask questions of the experts whenever I don't understand. Even though that twelve-year-old girl still lives on in my heart of hearts, and there are days she still buys on impulse—and, occasionally, when money's tight, she feels scared and longs for some man to take care of her so she doesn't have to be the responsible one—the result has been that I've gained some small understanding of finance and a greater sense of financial purpose.

Focusing your attention . . .

On the following pages, I am going to be asking you to begin filling in the blanks, identifying what you own and what you owe. I encourage you to make this experience as pleasant as possible. Put on your favorite music. Sit at a table that's been cleared for this purpose—except for, perhaps, a vase of flowers. Have a cup of tea or a cold drink beside you. Use colored pencils to write the information down. Relax. Focus your attention on identifying your precise financial circumstances. Remember, there is no time schedule here but yours. You can leave and come back to this process as often as you like.

As you work, you might want to place this reminder somewhere where you can look at it often to remind yourself of your goals:

My Goals for Understanding My Finances

❁ I want to be conscious about my financial resources.

❁ I want my spiritual life to enter my financial picture.

❁ I am looking for the points where my financial life and my spiritual life intersect.

What do you own? . . .

My assets

LIQUID ASSETS

(cash, or cash equivalents that can be exchanged for cash immediately)

Cash $ _____

(cash on hand, checking and savings accounts)

Money Market Funds _____

(like a checking account with some restrictions,

usually pays interest)

CD's (Certificates of Deposit) _____

(bank deposit with specified interest rate and date of maturity;

if you cash in ahead of time, there is usually a penalty)

Life Insurance – Personal _____

(cash value only)

TOTAL LIQUID ASSETS $ _____

My assets

NEAR LIQUID ASSETS
(investments that can be sold for cash in a few days)

Government Bonds/Corporate Bonds $_____

(investments that pay a fixed rate of return)

Municipal Bonds   _____

(fixed rate of return; not taxed)

Listed Stocks   _____

(stocks listed on the major stock exchanges; gives you
ownership in a company; value of the stock each day
is printed in the newspaper, on the Internet, and
financial TV channels)

Mutual Funds   _____

(stocks or other investment vehicles bundled into groups;
shares are sold representing a portion of the total value)

Other   _____

TOTAL NEAR LIQUID ASSETS $ _____

RETIREMENT ASSETS

Vested Pension $_____

(established by your employer; after a specified time, or vesting term, you are allowed to take it with you if you leave)

401-K Plans _____

(retirement savings plan for corporate employees)

403-B Plans _____

(retirement savings plan for nonprofit corporation employees)

IRAs (Individual Retirement Accounts) _____

(retirement savings under your control, established in a place of your choice)

SEP (Simplified Employee Pension) _____

(essentially an IRA set up by your employer)

Keogh _____

(retirement plan for self-employed)

Annuities _____

(an insurance investment vehicle purchased to provide a stream of income at retirement.)

Non-Qualified Deferred Compensation _____

(earnings not yet paid to you by your employer)

Other _____

TOTAL RETIREMENT ASSETS $_____

My assets

My assets

OTHER ASSETS

Non-Marketable Stocks & Bonds $_____

(not readily salable and not registered on the

major exchanges)

Equity in Business   _____

(share of a business that you own)

Your Home   _____

(estimated current market value)

Seasonal Residence   _____

(summer house, ski house, other residence you own and use)

Real Estate Investments   _____

Notes Receivable   _____

(money owed to you that you can reasonably expect to receive)

Automobiles   _____

(estimated current value)

Household Items   _____

(estimated value of furniture and fixtures in your home

if sold at a yard sale)

Jewelry and Other Precious Items   _____

Collections   _____

(antiques, books, whatever you collect that has value

individually and as a whole collection)

Other   _____

<u>TOTAL OTHER ASSETS</u> $_____

What do you owe ? . . .

LIABILITIES

Mortgage – Residential $_____

Home Equity Line of Credit   _____

Mortgage on Other Properties   _____

Car Loan(s)   _____

Student Loan(s)   _____

Credit Card Debt   _____

Store Debt and Other Forms of Debt Incurred
By Use of 'Plastic' Cards   _____

College Tuition   _____

Other Notes Payable   _____
(any type of note you've signed agreeing
to pay for something.)

TOTAL LIABILITIES $_____

My liabilities

My net worth

Putting it all together . . .

TOTAL ASSETS

Total Liquid Assets
(from pg 103)

$_____

Total Near Liquid Assets
(from pg 104)

_____

Total Retirement Assets
(from pg 105)

_____

Total Other Assets
(from pg 106)

_____

TOTAL ASSETS

_____

LESS: TOTAL LIABILITIES
(from pg 107)

— _____

NET WORTH

$ _____

What are you worth? . . .

There, you've done it! You have collected the basic financial facts of your life. One of my favorite cartoons about finances and people's reaction to them shows a group of well-dressed people sitting around a dinner table. The caption reads, "Money Is Life's Report Card." But, unlike school, you get to create your OWN report card, and there are no failing grades.

Yet, for many people, their "net worth" implies "success" or "failure." Sometimes people confuse their self-worth with their net worth. If they have a lot of money, they feel great. If they don't, they belittle themselves.

Think about these two terms: NET WORTH and SELF-WORTH. Is your sense of self-worth affected by the details of your net worth? Note some of your thoughts here:

My self-worth

The question is not whether you have too much money, or too little to meet even your monthly expenses. While it is important to manage your money well if you have it, and to stay out of debt if you don't have enough, neither is what the essence of your being is about.

As a wonderful antidote to the "net worth equals self-worth" mentality, you might find Henri Nouwen's book *Life of the Beloved* helpful. Believing that we are created out of love and are loved, Nouwen suggests taking time to ponder this thought and let it permeate our being.

Connect with your feelings . . .

As you have been working in this chapter to identify your financial facts, you have probably begun to identify your feelings about those facts. Your feelings about these important issues of life are where you and your spiritual beliefs come together, where you find your truth.

Sometimes an emotional moment in the midst of documents and dollar signs can open doors.

I am reminded of the scene in the Bible when Jesus sees the moneychangers in the temple and erupts in anger. I think this moment was not so much about being angry as it was about his core beliefs regarding the sacredness of God's house and the place of money. Sometimes an emotional moment in the midst of documents and dollar signs can open doors to deeper beliefs.

As you have been uncovering the financial facts of your life, you may have a stronger reaction to some items on your "assets and liabilities" lists than to others. For example, when I have money in my checking account, I feel good.

When I am close to the cash reserve, I am frightened. Is one place closer to the spiritual core than another? Why should my checking account balance influence my feelings about myself? I'm not sure why, but I know it does. The important thing is to acknowledge these feelings as I work with my financial facts.

Make a list of each type of account that seems to provoke a strong feeling in you. Write the dollar amount for each and a comment about your feelings. The following are samples of some comments I have heard women make:

My feelings

FINANCIAL FACT		FEELING
IRA		*Surprise:*
$ _____		*I have all this!*
	OR...	*Fear: It's not enough.*
Investment		*Embarrassment:*
$_____		*Don't know about it.*
	OR...	*Frustration:*
		Don't understand all this!
Credit card debt		*Fear:*
$_____		*How will I repay it?*
	OR...	*Anger: How did this happen?*

My feelings

Remember: There is no "right" or "wrong" when it comes to feelings. Feelings are important clues about what lies at your core.

FINANCIAL FACT	FEELING

A helping hand . . .

When I reflect on my early years of being a "grown-up"—
a working woman, a wife, mother, and then a single
parent—I wish I had had a mentor or a friend who would
have walked beside me on the journey into fiscal responsibility. As an only child, I embarked on a long, lonely learning through many courses, conversations, and experiences.
Perhaps you, too, are feeling lonely on this money journey.

**Do you feel like you need more support? Or do you need
people who are affected by your decisions to participate in this
process with you? If so, write down the names of people you
would like to be with you on this journey. Then put their
contact information next to the names.**

NAME   PHONE NUMBER   E-MAIL

My support

You can include other people in your work in a variety of ways:

❀ Simply contact a person on your list and tell her (or him) that you are working on your financial facts. Explain why it is hard for you and ask her to simple be a listener, or to take a break with you.

❀ Share with someone the joy that you are experiencing in beginning to take charge of your finances.

❀ Talk to a person who is central to the decisions you are making. Ask him or her for input.

❀ Invite others to create a group with you to share in the process of the money spirituality journey.

❀ Let others know about emotions that may be surfacing for you. Finances can often bring up emotions that you can't quite identify, and other people can offer support. Sometimes that happens just before a break-through or a new understanding.

At the precise moment you feel most vulnerable, you may be coming into your power.

Remember: At the precise moment you feel most vulnerable, you may be coming into your power. Once you know the story of your financial plusses and minuses, once you give yourself the authority to be in charge, there's no turning back to ignorance. You are giving yourself a gift and allowing yourself to replace negative messages with a sense of power and competence.

Call in the experts . . .

As you have collected your information, have you found holes? Perhaps you've never hired an accountant or an attorney before. Or maybe you haven't appointed anyone a power of attorney or health care proxy.

If someone in your life—husband, child, parent, friend—is taking care of your finances for you, you might feel that hiring financial help would be "betraying" them. Ask yourself: "Is the person currently monitoring my finances doing such a good job that I don't even have to PEEK at what's going on?"

Or perhaps there is nobody in charge. I've heard some women say that if they take their decisions about their money into their own hands, they have the sense of "falling from grace." Are you concerned that if you take charge, God will let go?

Here are some questions to consider:

- Can I manage my money myself?

- Can I let someone else do it entirely?

- Can I work in partnership with a professional or other knowledgeable, caring person?

If you think professional help may be a good idea for you, get recommendations from friends or a local professional society. Interview anyone you are considering. It is normal practice in these fields. You are not "wasting" someone's time. Professionals expect to spend some time discussing their approach, their credentials, and, of course, their fees. Here are some simple guidelines:

Guidelines for Getting Financial Help

❀ Take your time. Do not make hasty decisions.

❀ Research your choices.

❀ Seek references and referrals for all professionals you consider hiring.

❀ Interview someone before engaging his or her services.

❀ Pay attention to your intuitive guidance.

❀ Be sure the professional you choose understands your values and will honor them in the work you do together.

I had to learn how to choose a professional by choosing the wrong one first. I paid his bill and moved on until I found a professional I liked and could work with well. Making mistakes is part of any learning process. Allow yourself room for this to happen and count it as part of the cost of your "financial education."

Recap . . .

This chapter has focused on empowerment through knowl-edge of both your MONEY FACTS & FEELINGS. It has also encouraged you to take charge of your financial life. You have done a lot of the work of organizing your finances, but at this moment you may not yet have a sense of accomplish-ment or a feeling of peace. You may still be experiencing an uneasiness, almost a foreboding, that comes with walking into the unknown—especially if you were previously unaware of the total financial picture for you and your family.

Continue to trust your intuition. And continue to describe your feelings. What matters is that you are intentionally seeking knowledge and clarity of your financial affairs.

Take a minute here to note how you are feeling about being on this spiritual money journey. Do you feel any different than you did when you first decided to uncover your financial facts?

My feelings

Chapter Four

Creating Alignment

Moving on . . .

You have come a long way! You now have an understanding of what kind of messages have been reaching your consciousness since you were born. You have identified some of your resistance to organizing your finances. You've developed support by using this book and linking to other women. You have gathered together essential data. You have a special space to store your information. You have recorded your financial facts in a clear, readable format. You are well on your way to a new financial awareness that will be beneficial in ways you haven't even discovered yet. It is all to a powerful purpose: to bring your financial reality into an alignment with a larger, spiritual reality—who you are, what you care about, and how you want to live your life. This stage of The Money Journey Circle is the stage of ALIGNMENT: integrating your facts, feelings, and actions with your spiritual core.

The Money Journey Circle

"There is guidance for each of us, and by lowly listening, we shall hear the right word. Certainly there is a right for you that needs no choice on your part. Place yourself in the middle of the stream of power and wisdom which flows into your life."

—*Ralph Waldo Emerson,*
SPIRITUAL LAWS

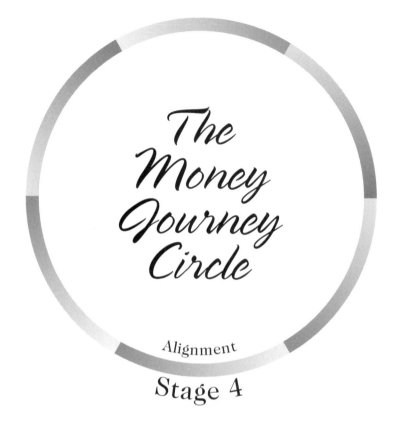

The Money Journey Circle

Alignment

Stage 4

The timing of alignment...

A few years ago, I led a workshop for a group of women entrepreneurs. Even though it might not have seemed like it at the time—since I was situated in a bland conference room in a nondescript office building on a chilly November afternoon—I can see now that I was in the middle of the "stream of power and wisdom," as Ralph Waldo Emerson so elegantly described it.

But alignment is like that. It doesn't necessarily show up as a glamorous moment, but as the coming together of intention and action, wherever and whenever that happens. And when our alignment connects with the alignment of other people who are seeking purposes that intersect with ours, that really makes the synchronicity happen!

One of the participants in that November workshop was a journalist named Joanne Kabak. She was there because she wanted to increase the income from her writing so that it would more fairly match her growing skills and reflect the economics of the current marketplace. She had returned to work to build a career as a journalist. Previously, she had been a CPA and then had stopped working to raise her children. Now that the kids were older, she wanted to contribute more financially to her household and to share the burden of the mortgage, impending college tuitions, and all the multiple expenses of living an active family life today. And she wanted to do it without compromising her intention to write about what was valuable and meaningful.

My intention for the workshop was to help women "prosper" in every sense of the word. I wanted to help other women come to grips with their finances and move beyond current monetary needs to their core desires and their spiritual "call." I wanted to encourage them to listen to and act on their inner voice that tries to be heard above the din of the material world. What had not left my mind during this process was that I still had a dream unfulfilled: to write about my work, my beliefs, and my hopes for women's breakthrough in money matters. I needed a teacher in order to do that writing.

Alignment doesn't necessarily show up as a glamorous moment, but as the coming together of intention and action.

121

Enter the journalist, Joanne, who happened to be in my small group. As she expressed her desire to write, teach her craft, and earn money from those skills, her goals joined up with my intention to communicate my message with clarity. We entered the "stream of power and wisdom" together at that moment, starting a relationship that has taken us through many articles and now this book.

As you consciously bring your actions in line with your spirit, things happen.

The funny thing is, we had met a couple of times before, when Joanne was a journalist at a local newspaper and I was designing and conducting seminars on women and money for that paper. She even interviewed me and wrote about me. But our intentions were not in line at that time… not until we met again at the right moment.

That's the way alignment often works. As you consciously bring your actions in line with your spirit, things happen without being forced, sometimes without being noticed until later. What starts to come through is something like the "lightness of being" you sometimes feel after good exercise or an inspiring concert. And you feel yourself being gently blown as by a soft wind into a new place, project, or perspective.

Consider for a moment your timing. What is happening in your life at this juncture that made you decide to pick up this book? Why are you interested in looking at your finances at this particular time? The answers are part of the story of your alignment. Take a few moments to consider this question:

Why are you focusing on money and spirituality now? What drew you to this process at this time in your life?

My timing

The flow of money . . .

The previous chapter focused on the "state" of your finances. Your list of assets and liabilities is a relatively stationary financial fact as of a certain date. It's like a snapshot of your finances.

In the next stage of your Money Journey, I am going to ask you to look at the "flow," how money comes in and goes out. Cash flow is more like a personal video of your financial life.

I believe understanding your cash flow is an essential ingredient in reaching alignment. It is like one of those levelers that carpenters use, a measure that tells you if you are off the mark of achieving balance, and if so, how far.

A cash flow statement, prepared carefully, honestly, and with enough detail, can let you know whether or not your CASH IN is equal to your CASH OUT. It informs you about the amount you may be overspending, or the amount of discretionary income you have left over after expenses. And it provides you with the hard evidence you need to answer a critical question: "Am I spending my money wisely and well, the way I want to, or am I spending money habitually, on things I don't really care about?"

Why? . . .

You might be asking, "Do I really need to do all the work of creating a cash flow statement? What do I need to know all those numbers for?"

I can think of at least four reasons why it is helpful to prepare a cash flow:

❀ To get clear about the sources of your money and the ways in which you spend it.

❀ To get clear about your values.

❀ To reflect on your money flow and your values together.

❀ To begin the lifelong process of bringing your money and your spiritual life in line with each other.

Convergence . . .

I want to tell you about a woman named Sue Roselle. When she examined her spending, she saw that there were major cash outflows going to her hometown of Pittsburgh: six airfares in a year, big phone bills, contributions to her home church. She realized that even though her body—and her job—were in Chicago, her heart and soul were in Pittsburgh.

At the same time, she was feeling repeated disappointment about her job and her company. That discontent hit home one day when she felt she really needed someone to talk to about her job. She realized she didn't have anyone to call in Chicago. She had been so intent on her work that she had forgotten to make friends!

What good was a six-figure salary if it meant an eighty-hour week, and a lack of friends, family, social relationships? She took the time to ask herself, "What do I really want in life? What is important to me?"

The convergence of her money facts, her discontent, her attention to her soul's needs, and her connection to her family brought her into a place of alignment. She stopped sacrificing the personal for the professional and returned to Pittsburgh for the pleasures of having her family nearby and living a simpler lifestyle. She found a new job with people she respects—at half her salary—but now her eyes glow with a deep satisfaction when she smiles and talks about her life.

Know the flow . . .

Your checkbook, credit cards, tax returns, bills, day planner, and computer files can provide the information of your daily financial life. They tell you where you've been, what you've done, how much it cost to be there, and what you've brought home. They tell you about the transactions you enter into, day by day.

If you dig a little deeper, you will see this data also tells you what you enjoy, how you stay healthy, what is important to you. Your priorities are crystal clear in these records. Become comfortable looking at your bank statements and your bills, not just as items to check off, but as the story of your life.

To help you prepare your own cash flow statement, I have included two different cash flow forms to choose from. You can decide on the level of detail you want and work with the form that fits you best:

VERSION 1: Detail Cash Flow (pages 130-135)
To get lots of facts, you can review your finances for one complete year on a 12-month form. Enter the money you received and the money you spent in the appropriate months. For example, dividends are usually paid quarterly, so you would enter this income in the four appropriate months of the year. Salaries, on the other hand, may come in on a weekly or biweekly basis, and bonuses on an annual basis. Some expenditures are weekly (such as food), monthly (such as the mortgage or rent), quarterly (such as insurance bills), or annually (such as taxes). Entering these facts in the month in which they occur will give you a more accurate financial picture.

VERSION 2: Summary Cash Flow (pages 136-138)
If, on the other hand, you are not concerned with this level of detail, you can prepare a more simplified cash flow. Estimate one month's income and expenses and then multiply this by 12 to get an average yearly picture.

Getting ready . . .

Whichever form you choose, preparing a cash flow statement is an important step in bringing your financial and spiritual values into alignment. It may require some work, but it does not have to be unpleasant. Here are a few suggestions of ways you can make it easier and more fun:

❦ You might want to copy the cash flow form you choose onto colored paper—sunny yellow or lavender are two of my favorites. Colors help many women overcome their aversion to working with black-and-white columns of numbers.

❦ Personalize the form. Are there items not on the form that you want to include, or items to eliminate? This is YOUR story, and it is different from anyone else's. I have identified only basic categories. You probably have other ones that are specific to your lifestyle. Add them to the form.

❦ You may want to use colored pens and pencils to record your numbers.

❦ Choose a happy place to do the work. Play music. Be comfortable. Let the sunshine in.

❦ Plan a special time to do this. Otherwise you may keep putting it off. Plan something pleasing to do afterward, and think up rewards along the way.

Before you start, I want to recommend you do one thing: Place the following page where you can review it often to remind yourself of WHY YOU ARE DOING THIS WORK and WHAT IT CAN TELL YOU.

What My Cash Flow Can Tell Me

❁ How I take in money.

❁ For what reasons, or under what circumstances, I release that money back out into
the world (in other words, spend it).

❁ What my true necessities are.

❁ If I am living at, above, or below my income.

❁ What I really care about.

❁ Where my money flow and my values are in
harmony.

❁ If I am using my money for what is important
to me.

❁ What changes I could realistically make to
bring my money closer to where my
spirit lives.

The ins and outs of money . . .

My cash flow

VERSION 1: DETAIL CASH FLOW

	Jan	Feb	Mar	April
INCOME				
Income#1 (before tax withholdings)	—	—	—	—
Income #2 (before tax withholdings)	—	—	—	—
Bonus	—	—	—	—
Dividends				
From stocks	—	—	—	—
From money market funds	—	—	—	—
Interest				
From treasury bills and notes or other government issues	—	—	—	—
From saving accounts	—	—	—	—
From other sources (such as municipal bonds or personal loans)	—	—	—	—
Additional income				
From pensions	—	—	—	—
From trust funds	—	—	—	—
From rents/real estate	—	—	—	—
Social security income	—	—	—	—
Income from partnerships or other business investments	—	—	—	—
Sales of securities	—	—	—	—
Other income from whatever source	—	—	—	—
TOTAL INCOME	—	—	—	—

My cash flow

May	June	July	Aug	Sept	Oct	Nov	Dec	YEAR
—	—	—	—	—	—	—	—	—
—	—	—	—	—	—	—	—	—
—	—	—	—	—	—	—	—	—
—	—	—	—	—	—	—	—	—
—	—	—	—	—	—	—	—	—
—	—	—	—	—	—	—	—	—
—	—	—	—	—	—	—	—	—
—	—	—	—	—	—	—	—	—
—	—	—	—	—	—	—	—	—
—	—	—	—	—	—	—	—	—
—	—	—	—	—	—	—	—	—
—	—	—	—	—	—	—	—	—
—	—	—	—	—	—	—	—	—
—	—	—	—	—	—	—	—	—
—	—	—	—	—	—	—	—	—

My cash flow

VERSION 1: cont'd

	Jan	Feb	Mar	April
NECESSARY EXPENDITURES				
Mortgage/rent	—	—	—	—
Food/groceries	—	—	—	—
Utilities/telephone	—	—	—	—
Home maintenance	—	—	—	—
Clothing/cleaning	—	—	—	—
Personal needs	—	—	—	—
Transportation expenses	—	—	—	—
Medical/dental	—	—	—	—
Insurance payments				
Medical	—	—	—	—
Disability	—	—	—	—
Life	—	—	—	—
Car	—	—	—	—
Personal Property	—	—	—	—
Other	—	—	—	—
Credit cards	—	—	—	—
Debt/loans	—	—	—	—
Taxes				
Real estate	—	—	—	—
Personal property or other state/local tax	—	—	—	—
Estimated income tax payments	—	—	—	—
Payroll deductions/tax payments				
Federal/State	—	—	—	—
Social Security	—	—	—	—
Medicare	—	—	—	—
Other	—	—	—	—
TOTAL NECESSARY EXPENDITURES	—	—	—	—

May	June	July	Aug	Sept	Oct	Nov	Dec	**YEAR**
—	—	—	—	—	—	—	—	—
—	—	—	—	—	—	—	—	—
—	—	—	—	—	—	—	—	—
—	—	—	—	—	—	—	—	—
—	—	—	—	—	—	—	—	—
—	—	—	—	—	—	—	—	—
—	—	—	—	—	—	—	—	—
—	—	—	—	—	—	—	—	—
—	—	—	—	—	—	—	—	—
—	—	—	—	—	—	—	—	—
—	—	—	—	—	—	—	—	—
—	—	—	—	—	—	—	—	—
—	—	—	—	—	—	—	—	—
—	—	—	—	—	—	—	—	—
—	—	—	—	—	—	—	—	—
—	—	—	—	—	—	—	—	—
—	—	—	—	—	—	—	—	—
—	—	—	—	—	—	—	—	—
—	—	—	—	—	—	—	—	—
—	—	—	—	—	—	—	—	—

My cash flow

My cash flow

VERSION 1: cont'd

	Jan	Feb	Mar	April
DISCRETIONARY EXPENDITURES				
Vacations/travel	—	—	—	—
Recreation	—	—	—	—
Entertainment	—	—	—	—
Dining out	—	—	—	—
Contributions	—	—	—	—
Gifts	—	—	—	—
Family support	—	—	—	—
Household furnishings	—	—	—	—
Home improvements	—	—	—	—
Pets	—	—	—	—
Education funding	—	—	—	—
Savings	—	—	—	—
Investments	—	—	—	—
Other	—	—	—	—
Other	—	—	—	—
Other	—	—	—	—
TOTAL DISCRETIONARY EXPENDITURES	—	—	—	—

My cash flow

May	June	July	Aug	Sept	Oct	Nov	Dec	**YEAR**
—	—	—	—	—	—	—	—	—
—	—	—	—	—	—	—	—	—
—	—	—	—	—	—	—	—	—
—	—	—	—	—	—	—	—	—
—	—	—	—	—	—	—	—	—
—	—	—	—	—	—	—	—	—
—	—	—	—	—	—	—	—	—
—	—	—	—	—	—	—	—	—
—	—	—	—	—	—	—	—	—
—	—	—	—	—	—	—	—	—
—	—	—	—	—	—	—	—	—
—	—	—	—	—	—	—	—	—
—	—	—	—	—	—	—	—	—
—	—	—	—	—	—	—	—	—
—	—	—	—	—	—	—	—	—
—	—	—	—	—	—	—	—	—

MY SUMMARY

MY INCOME _____

MY NECESSARY EXPENDITURES — _____

MY DISCRETIONARY EXPENDITURES — _____

MY NET CASH FLOW _____

My cash flow

VERSION 2: SUMMARY CASH FLOW

INCOME	Average Month	YEAR
Income #1	_____	_____
(before tax withholdings)		
Income #2	_____	_____
(before tax withholdings)		
Bonus	_____	_____
Dividends		
From stocks	_____	_____
From money market funds	_____	_____
Interest		
From treasury bills and notes or other government issues	_____	_____
From saving accounts	_____	_____
From other sources (such as municipal bonds or personal loans)	_____	_____
Additional income		
From pensions	_____	_____
From trust funds	_____	_____
From rents/real estate	_____	_____
Social Security income	_____	_____
Income from partnerships or other business investments	_____	_____
Sales of securities	_____	_____
Other income from whatever source	_____	_____
TOTAL INCOME	_____	_____

VERSION 2: cont'd

NECESSARY EXPENDITURES	Average Month	YEAR
Mortgage/rent	_____	_____
Food/groceries	_____	_____
Utilities/telephone	_____	_____
Home maintenance	_____	_____
Clothing/cleaning	_____	_____
Personal needs	_____	_____
Transportation expenses	_____	_____
Medical/dental	_____	_____
Insurance payments		
Medical	_____	_____
Disability	_____	_____
Life	_____	_____
Car	_____	_____
Personal Property	_____	_____
Other	_____	_____
Credit cards	_____	_____
Debt/loans	_____	_____
Taxes		
Real estate	_____	_____
Personal property or other state/local tax	_____	_____
Estimated income tax payments	_____	_____
Payroll deductions/tax payments		
Federal/State	_____	_____
Social Security	_____	_____
Medicare	_____	_____
Other	_____	_____
TOTAL NECESSARY EXPENDITURES	_____	_____

My cash flow

My cash flow

VERSION 2: cont'd

DISCRETIONARY EXPENDITURES	Average Month	YEAR
Vacations/travel	_____	____
Recreation	_____	____
Entertainment	_____	____
Dining out	_____	____
Contributions	_____	____
Gifts	_____	____
Family support	_____	____
Household furnishings	_____	____
Home improvements	_____	____
Pets	_____	____
Education funding	_____	____
Savings	_____	____
Investments	_____	____
Other	_____	____
Other	_____	____
Other	_____	____
TOTAL DISCRETIONARY EXPENDITURES	_____	____

MY SUMMARY

MY INCOME _____

MY NECESSARY EXPENDITURES — _____

MY DISCRETIONARY EXPENDITURES — _____

MY NET CASH FLOW _____

What do the numbers tell you?...

Now that you have done the work of preparing a cash flow statement, the next step is to figure out what all these numbers tell you. What can you learn from this numerical picture of your financial life?

One by one, prayerfully consider the following six questions:

1. How do you feel about the cash flow statement you have created?

2. Are there changes you need to make?

For example, are all your health care needs taken care of, or are you putting them off because you feel you don't have the money?

My assessment

3. Are there any changes you want to make?
For example, if you are taking in more money than you need, would you like to give some away?

4. What are some of the discretionary categories that take a measurable chunk of your money?

5. Are your earnings at a level that reflects the value of your work and your belief system?

My assessment

6. Do you see any spending that needs re-evaluating?

A balancing act ...

In simple terms, alignment is balancing our needs and wants with our values and goals.

Inherent in the very design of the human being is the yearning for alignment—the coming together of desire, intention, action, and result.

Teilhard de Chardin speaks of the intertwining of all our experiences, feelings, and intellect with the external circumstances of our daily life. At the time that Teilhard lived, DNA was not part of the scientific vocabulary. But I believe he was talking about something close to a spiritual DNA, a God-essence that is in our very cells.

Your financial life is not a solo instrument. It is not separate and distinct from the orchestra of who you are.

When our mind, body, and spirit are in alignment, at that moment we are acting out of our God-essence. Think of alignment as an orchestra. If all the "players," i.e., mind, body, and spirit, are playing in tune, the music is harmonious. But if one section is "off key," the whole orchestra sounds out of tune.

What I am suggesting is that your financial life is not a solo instrument. It is not separate and distinct from the orchestra of who you are—although it may feel that way when you look only at balance sheets and check books. How you use your money and resources is an integral part of your essence.

What's important to you? . . .

I am going to ask you to set aside your cash flow statement for a moment and take some time to focus on what you want, as well your discontents.

Like Sue, the Chicago woman who moved to Pittsburgh, do you have times when you're working long hours and not having enough time for relationships? Do you ever find yourself thinking about living your life with less money but more satisfaction, and then the image leaves you and you go back to your tasks?

In my case, it's often the images that I have from my travels to Haiti that cause my greatest discontent. I know that many a child in that country could be educated but isn't— all for lack of the eighty dollars to pay for a year's worth of schooling. And then I find myself dropping forty dollars on flowers for my front doorstep.

Yet when I put the flowers out, my memory flashes immediately back to a scene in Sarajevo. When I visited the city in 1996, I stood in the courtyard of an apartment complex that had survived serious bombing. Not all the buildings were intact, but each of those that were had balconies supporting window boxes with cascades of flowers. It created a visual smorgasbord of color—a nourishment for the eye and the heart. I felt the link between my peaceful home in the suburbs of the U.S. and this city torn up by mindless warfare. The contrast couldn't have been more extreme. In my own home, I want the same thing: the beauty and peace that lovely flowers can bring.

> "I began to wonder: suppose I were hit by a Mack truck tomorrow; how would my check-book stubs reflect what I cared about?"
>
> —Gloria Steinem,
> MOVING BEYOND

Sue experienced alignment when she moved back to Pittsburgh and rearranged her life. I experience alignment when I lead trips to Haiti to initiate micro-lending projects. And I also experience it when I recognize that I am spending money on flowers to acknowledge beauty and to bring a moment of joy to myself and to my neighbors, who often remark what a pleasure it is to see the pansies in bloom.

What is important to you? The following four questions will help you assess whether your use of money is in line with what you really care about.

My alignment

1. What do you want? What do you care about for yourself, your family, your neighborhood or city, the global community? Don't be concerned about whether each item is a reality in your life. Simply ask yourself, "What am I really passionate about?"

2. Now list some of your discontents. What do you see that isn't working in your own life, or in the larger world? What would you want to change if you could?

My alignment

3. What part of your cash flow is in line with what you really care about?

4. What part of your cash flow seems to be in conflict with what you really care about?

Recap ...

A friend of mine continues to tell me, "Pay attention to the details; God is in the details."

This chapter has certainly brought you face-to-face with the financial details of your life. I hope the cash flow exercise has given you a deeper awareness of your economic habits and attitudes. If so, it has accomplished its task of calling your attention to the details that shape your financial life. The question I have asked you to consider is whether your financial life is in ALIGNMENT with your spiritual values, with what matters most to you.

Think about this statement for a moment: "Each detail, each financial decision, has the potential to bring my attention to other possible alternatives."

I believe this is true. There is the potential in each deciding moment to make a choice that is different from our habitual behavior. But I also believe that, when we are out moving about in our economic lives, it is too late to begin to think about the actions we want to take. We need to become aware and decide on our actions in the quiet of our deepest self, where God is.

Bring your heightened personal financial awareness to prayer as you consider what is next for you on your Money Journey.

Ending prayer . . .

In silence, God,

I share now my eagerness

and my uneasiness

about this something different

I would be or do;

And I listen for your leading

to help me separate

the light from the darkness

in the change I seek to shape

and which is shaping me.

—*Ted Loder, GUERRILLAS OF GRACE*

Resources . . .

BOOKS

The 9 Steps to Financial Freedom, Suze Orman (New York: Crown, 1997).
> This book provides good basic financial planning information.

Money and the Meaning of Life, Jacob Needleman (New York: Doubleday, 1994).
> A philosopher offers interesting thoughts on the philosophy underlying the use of money.

When Corporations Rule the World, David C. Korten (San Francisco: Berrett-Koehler, 1996).
> This book explores the emerging global system of business as a threat to human beings.

The Motley Fool Investment Guide; How the Fools Beat Wall Street's Wise Men and How You Can Too, David Gardner, Tom Gardner. (New York: Fireside, 1997).
> A guide to investing based on the theories of the Gardner brothers. They are the authors and creators of the "Motley Fool" image—a court jester who is the only individual in the royal court who can get away with telling the king the truth—as a symbol of their straight talk, with humor, about money.

The Motley Fool Investment Workbook, David Gardner, Tom Gardner. (New York: Fireside, 1998).
> Charts, graphs, questionnaires, and quizzes to help investors identify resources and develop investment strategies. (Note: Motley Fool materials are also available on tape.)

The Energy of Money, Maria Nemeth (New York: Ballantine, 1997).
> A good resource book for those who want to explore personal motivations regarding money management.

Invested in the Common Good, Susan Meeker-Lowery (Gabriola Island, British Columbia: New Society Publishers, 1995).

> An excellent introduction to socially conscious investing information.

Life of the Beloved: Spiritual Living in a Secular World, Henri J.M. Nouwen (New York: Crossroad, 1997).

> A remarkable aspect of this book is that while Nouwen is writing to a personal friend, he in fact has found a language that speaks clearly and convincingly to all who search for the Spirit of God in the world.

FINANCIAL NEWSLETTERS

Green Money Journal
608 West Glass Avenue
Spokane, WA 99205
509-328-1741
www.greenmoney.com

> This journal promotes the awareness of socially and environmentally responsible business, investing, and consumer resources. Their goal is to educate and empower individuals and businesses to make informed financial decisions.

Women's Philanthropy Institute News
6314 Odana Road, Suite 1
Madison, WI 53719-2052
608-270-5205
www.women-philanthropy.org

> This newsletter of Women's Philanthropy Institute educates and encourages women to effect positive change as major donors and volunteer leaders for the nonprofit causes of their choosing.

More Than Money (publication office)
2244 Alder Street
Eugene, OR 97405
800-255-4903

More Than Money (organization office)
226 Massachusetts Avenue
Arlington, MA 02474
781-648-0776
www.morethanmoney.org
> This quarterly publication is written for people questioning society's assumptions about money, and particularly for those with inherited or earned wealth seeking a more joyful, just, and sustainable world.

CONFERENCES

Everywoman's Money Conference
Project Green Purse
5665 SW Meadows Road, Suite 260
Lake Oswego, OR 97035
503-624-9446
www.greenpurse.com
> Project Green Purse offers one-day conferences in major cities across the country to educate and empower women financially.

WEBSITES

www.fool.com
> The website of the Motley Fool is created by an organization dedicated to educating people about money and finance.
>   The Motley Fool
>   123 N. Pitt Street
>   Alexandria, VA 22314
>   703-838-3665

www.smartmoney.com

> A website from SmartMoney, a financial magazine
> published jointly by Dow Jones and Hearst, that
> covers all major financial issues.
>> SmartMoney
>> 1755 Broadway, 2nd Floor
>> New York, NY 10019
>> 800-444-4204

www.individualinvestor.com

> This is a website of the Individual Investor Magazine,
> a monthly publication of the Individual Investor
> Group, Inc., that features analysis of financial issues
> relevant to the individual investor.
>> Individual Investor Letters
>> 125 Broad Street, 14th Floor
>> New York, NY 10004
>> 818-616-7677 (for subscriptions to the magazine)

www.ministryofmoney.org

> The Ministry of Money website is an excellent
> resource for people on a faith and money journey.
> The site feature programs, events, resource lists,
> newsletter information, and links to other articles
> on faith and money.
>> Ministry of Money
>> 11315 Neelsville Church Road
>> Germantown, MD 20876
>> 301-428-9560

www.womensperspective.org

> The Women's Perspective website focuses on the
> unique perspective that women bring to money and
> spirituality, and provides information about Women,
> Money & Spirituality workshops and about trips to
> economically deprived countries such as Haiti.
>> Women's Perspective
>> 421 Meadow Street
>> Fairfield, CT 06430
>> 203-336-2238

RESOURCES TO HELP YOU GET ORGANIZED

Organizing from the Inside Out, Julie Morgenstern
(New York: Henry Holt/Owl, 1998). (www.juliemorgenstern.com)
>A method of organizing based on your life's goals, habits, and psychological needs.

Creative Time Management for the New Millennium, Jan
Yager (Stamford, CT: Hannacroix Creek Books, Inc., 1999).
(www.jyanger.com)
>A time management guide that recognizes the hectic world we live in and gives specific advice on how to be more effective and creative in managing your time so you can be more productive.

Breathing Space, Jeff Davidson (Chapel Hill, NC: Breathing
Space, 2000). (www.breathingspace.com)
>This book is for people who feel like they are drowning in paper, information, etc. Suggests ways to get in control of your space so you can get in control of the rest of your life and feel more positive.

*Organize Your Home! Simple Routines for Managing Your
Household,* Ronni Eisenberg, Kate Kelly (New York:
Hyperion, 1999). (www.reisenberg.com)
>This book provides information on getting your house in order, including how to organize valuable papers.

The Joy of Simple Living, Jeff Davidson
(Emmaus, PA: Rodale Press, 1999).
>   Focuses on ways to unclutter and de-complicate your
>   life. Takes you drawer-by-drawer and room-by-room.

Homefile Publishing
10025 Gov. Warfield Pkwy
Suite 1-8
Columbia, MD
21044800-695-3453
www.organizerkits.com
>   This company sells helpful organizational materials for
>   filing financial information.

The National Association of Personal
Financial Advisors (NAPFA)
355 West Dundee Road, Suite 200
Buffalo Grove, IL 60089
847-537-7722
888-FEE-ONLY (888-333-6659)
www.napfa.org
>   This organization offers referrals to fee-only financial
>   planners in all areas of the country.

Part Three

Divine One, Spirit of Creation, open my mind to the possibility of call, the inner voice that whispers direction to me. Give me the ability to see, hear, feel, intuit, perceive, and know in some way the path that is open to me.

Enable me to overcome my blocks and my fears. Help me to understand that my resources—talents, money, and the blessings of family and friends—are part of the circle of love you provide for me.

Expand my vision to help me see that the difficulties and challenges of my life are my teachers. Enable me to receive them graciously.

Encourage me as I connect my financial resources to my spiritual resources. Shed a bright light so that the creative path of my life may become more obvious to me. Support me as the miracles of my life take shape.

This section will help you . . .

....

❁ Look for indications of call in your life.

❁ Bring to your consciousness patterns that point to a direction you might want to follow.

❁ Think outside the box. Open and expand your awareness to the possibilities that already exist or that you can create.

❁ Identify ways that you or your money could support that dream.

❁ Answer the question, "If I had complete freedom of choice, what would I choose to do?"

Chapter Five

Dream On

Seeing the future . . .

For many women today, their dreams are blocked by a seemingly insurmountable obstacle: MONEY. The ignorance of money, the fear of money, the lack of money.

One of my hopes in writing this book is to help you remove money as an obstacle and turn it into a comfortable companion to your spirit. So far, you have looked at money in many different ways:

- Identifying the messages you've heard about money.

- Recording your personal money auto-biography.

- Detailing how much money you have, where it comes from, and where it goes.

- Expressing what is important to you.

- Assessing whether your use of money is in line with what you really care about.

The Money Journey Circle

"If one advances confidently in the direction of [her] dreams and endeavors to live the life [she] has imagined, [she] will meet with a success unexpected in common hours."

—Henry David Thoreau,
ON WALDEN POND

Now that you've done the work of the previous chapters, it is time to link your finances with your inner dreams and outer actions. This fifth stage of The Money Journey Circle focuses on DREAMS, on opening yourself to the idea of "call," to the direction for which your life is intended. This is the stage of seeing your future as an expression of your dreams and desires.

"But I can't . . . "

There are many different ways—a vision, a personal experience, a "funny" feeling—in which a new direction can become known to you, but there is often a common response: "But I can't do that. I don't have the money, the courage, the knowledge, the ability... to start a new career, fund a program, learn a skill, make a difference."

Consider the following quote:

> *"The moment one definitely commits oneself, then providence moves too. All sorts of things occur to help one that would never have otherwise occurred. A whole stream of events issues from the decision raising in one's favor all manner of unforeseen incidents and meetings and material assistance which no one could have dreamed would come [her] way. Whatever you can do, or dream you can, begin it. Boldness has genius, power and magic in it.*
>
> *—ascribed to Wolfgang Goethe*

Even though in this chapter you will be putting aside your financial data for the moment, know that you are moving forward with a new understanding of your financial picture and your responses to it. With the confidence this understanding gives you, you are now ready to spend some time focusing on your soul's direction.

"Whatever you can do or dream, you can begin it. Boldness has genius, power and magic in it."

In the moment . . .

Life, both the visible and invisible, happens in the moment. Inspiration, grace, God—all of those and more happen right NOW. And we respond with all our history, inclinations, and potential of our being. The beauty of it is that each moment holds infinite possibility.

A friend once told me that I seemed like Lot's wife: "Rosemary, you are always looking backward." I became quite indignant and argued with her. But she continued, pointing out how many times I got stuck because I was recounting the past or reliving it. What had happened took precedence over what is happening.

The beauty of it is that each moment holds infinite possibility.

Then I began to experiment with the notion of life as the teacher—in each minute, throughout the day, in good moments and rough ones. Each day brought new opportunities to see myself more clearly, to walk intentionally, seeking direction moment by moment.

Each morning I asked for the grace to live the day consciously with awareness of events and people as a part of a much larger pattern. As I let myself become aware of the enormous power of the present moment, my inner and outer worlds entered a transformative process, and my calling in life became more obvious to me. The clues were all around me, and they began to form a thread that, when I let it, wove its way through my life. The thread took shape when, seemingly by happenstance, I learned of the Ministry of Money organization. From there, you already know the outcome of that thread: I became part of Ministry of Money and accepted an invitation to go to Haiti, and eventually became director of the Women's Perspective. Consider what you can do in a moment:

🌸 Acknowledge who you are.

🌸 Acknowledge what you have.

🌸 Acknowledge your feelings.

🌸 Recognize your tendencies.

🌸 Hold the truth of yourself clearly.

🌸 Be aware of what you are currently doing.

🌸 Actively ask for guidance.

Discovering your call . . .

In the lives of women I have worked with, and in the course of my own life, I have seen amazing transformations happen around the issues of money. Each woman approaches that transformation from a different place. Some are poised to put their money in alignment with their spirit and need only a little "nudge," a little more insight, a new sense of order to make the connection. Others have more work to do and find that they need more time to understand their finances before they can meld its uses with their spiritual energy.

But over and over, I have seen one consistent pattern: When people allow a dream to come to light, amazing "coincidences" do happen. Perhaps the best way to illustrate this is to simply tell brief stories of women who heeded a notion, a message, or a messenger.

Accidents happen . . .

I'll start with my daughter, Sharon Williams. She arrived at her sense of purpose literally by accident. At the end of a cross-country bicycle trip, she was seriously injured in an accident. The trip had been planned during a hiatus from college, at a time when she was looking for a career. She never expected a career to come out of the pain and trauma of a head-and-neck injury.

After she fell over the handle bars and hit her head, she was taken to a hospital. While she was seemingly unconscious, she later said she could see and hear all that was going on around her. At that moment, she made the choice to live and the commitment to healing.

As Sharon began to recover, she found she was not getting enough relief from the usual medical treatments available to her. That's when she went to an excellent chiropractor. Not only did she improve, she found her call: to enter the healing profession as a chiropractor.

As with many choices of the heart, the reality of money, finances, and the demands of the external world entered the picture. Sharon did not have the money to finish college and go on to graduate school to study to be a chiropractor. She knew well the issue of financial insecurity. She had seen first her father, then me, lose our "secure" corporate jobs over time.

But when a chosen path is in alignment with your soul, a way starts to emerge. For Sharon, that way took shape through borrowing money for school, my taking out a home equity loan, Sharon finding and buying a small house, renting out rooms to pay the loan, and supporting herself with the rental income, as well as living there. Although she continued to be afraid that she couldn't pay the loans back, the accident and its aftermath made her more willing to take risks, to make the commitment to serve in a healing profession, and to have the confidence to take on debt and the steps to pay it back.

Sharon is now a chiropractor with a successful practice, lives in her little house still, and continues to pay down her debt. All the while she is fulfilling her dream of helping people be healthier, both in body and spirit.

A story of faith . . .

I think of another woman, Anne Hastings. In her own words, Anne has said that her direction came from a nagging sense that there must be more to life, from a longing for more meaning. Rather than disregard that pull, Anne started to think about the Peace Corps and mentioned it to friends. Someone suggested she contact a Haitian priest, Father Joseph Fillipe. Father Joseph had a vision of starting a grassroots banking system in Haiti, and he had a dream that he could enlist someone who spoke French, Creole, and English, was a bank president or director, and could volunteer and be self-supporting for three years in Haiti.

Although Anne could not speak French or Creole, had no banking experience, and needed to be supported financially in order to do a volunteer year in Haiti, Father Fillipe still believed she was the right person. For her part, Anne said, "It just felt right." Funding for her first year came from friends of both Father Fillipe and Anne who were intrigued by the idea. She eventually found second-year funding by applying for grants to the San Carlos Foundation in Berkeley, California, which funds professionals for missionary work.

Anne is now in her fourth year in Haiti. Fonkoze, a peasant banking system she helped create, is up and running. And Fondwa, a model community in the mountains of Haiti, is a visible manifestation of the intangible dream of both Father Fillipe and Anne Hastings.

Among the many surprises along the way for Anne was that, when she entered this path, she did not have a vocabulary that included a language of faith. She was not particularly religious and her initial actions that led her to Haiti were not faith-based. She was primarily interested in simplifying her life. Now, after her amazing experiences, she speaks of the strong faith she has gained, learning "to let problematic things go, knowing answers will come."

A creative process . . .

My third story is about a woman named Charlotte Lyman Fardelmann. Her life is a beautiful example of how a change in relationship to money by just one person can affect many others.

A major financial fact in Charlotte's life was an inheritance that gave her a financial cushion. Accompanying this fact was an overriding feeling of discomfort, even guilt, over having more money and resources than the people around her. Where was the justice in that, she wondered?

Charlotte went from feeling apart from others because she didn't have the same money issues, to joining hands with other women who, like her, had also inherited money. Together they started the Lyman Fund, which gives small grants to applicants to take the next step on their spiritual journeys.

By having her own fund, Charlotte is not just an observer of the process of change, but a participant in making a difference through the use of money. So far, more than two hundred people have received grants from the Lyman Fund. Each year recipients are invited to a gathering to talk about the changes in their lives since receiving the grants. A community has begun among them, creating more spiritual energy. Her book, *Nudged by the Spirit: Stories of People Responding to the Still, Small Voice of God* tells the story of the dreams that have come to fruition with the help of seed money.

The catalyst for Charlotte was twofold: the work she did on her money issues and the work she did on her spiritual quest. Through study, workshops, and interaction with others who were focusing on a deeper understanding of money, she overcame her anxiety and transformed her thinking about her inheritance and the power it gave her. And through a prayerful and dedicated study within her faith community of Quakers, she found grounding for her spiritual journey as well as friends who worked with her to create the Lyman Fund. She describes her journey as a five-step creative process. You may find her steps resonate with yours:

Five-Step Creative Process

1. INPUT: "My childhood discomfort with the wealthy society world."
2. GESTATION: "Wrestling with the issue of money, learning about people's spiritual journeys, culminating with joining with my two friends to form the Lyman Fund."
3. SHARING: "The first seven years of grant giving."
4. GOING PUBLIC: "Celebrating with the grantees as Lyman Fund becomes an incorporated foundation."
5. MOVING ON: "Into the unknown, the beginning of the next cycle in the spiral."

She wouldn't take no for an answer . . .

The face of the five-pound note in Irish currency is a supreme example of a woman integrating financial and spiritual issues. On the note is a picture of Catherine McAuley, the founder of the Sisters of Mercy, a Catholic order of nuns. She started the order in her forties after she inherited a fortune from a childless couple she had befriended. In today's money the fortune would be worth about one million dollars. She wanted to use some of those resources to help the poor of Dublin.

Catherine enlisted the help of her friends, and they began to offer food and clothing to the poor of the city. The church authorities at the time told her she could not do the work she wanted because that work was done only by nuns. I like to imagine her saying to herself, "Okay. I'll start an order of nuns. And we will get this work of helping the poor done." Today the order continues Catherine's mission, and she is honored on the currency of Ireland.

Synergy . . .

The story of Julie Spahr is an example of the kind of synergy that can happen when two women living out their dream come together. Julie had decided to go back to college in mid-life to get her degree. She found it such a profound experience that she went on to complete a master's degree program at Temple University. It was an experience that launched a new career for her. Out of her desire to share her enthusiasm for education with other mid-life women who dreamed of going back to school for advanced degrees, she set up a scholarship fund for women through a community foundation.

Parallel to Julie's story is the story of Elin Danien, a seventy-year-old woman who completed a Ph.D. program at the University of Pennsylvania and founded a scholarship fund in 1986. She personally funded the first scholarship award in 1987. Julie was invited to join with Elin and others to establish a scholarship fund called Bread Upon the Water to help other Ph.D. candidates. When their purposes came together, these two women were able to create and participate in something larger than either one of them could have done by themselves.

What is your story? . . .

Call grows out of the composite of who we are in the world and the experiences we have had. To get a clearer picture, I have found it very helpful to take an inventory of my work history, for jobs paid or unpaid. Here's what I came up with when I did this exercise:

Baby-sitting

Picking beans and berries

Chores around the house

Selling hats in a department store

Summer job taking applications for working papers

Winter part-time job taking heat complaints for the health department of the City of New York

College part-time job modeling in department stores

Volunteer in a home for the elderly

Statistician for economic projections

Coordinator for sales force

Mother, wife, and homemaker

School and community volunteer

Sunday school teacher

Volunteer as public relations coordinator for nonprofit

Trust officer, loan officer, department manager, vice president of a commercial bank

Herb salesperson

Financial planner

Development consultant

Director of the Women's Perspective

Advocate for third-world women

Retreat and workshop leader

Educator

Author

My work history . . .

1. Now try this exercise for yourself. Make a list of the jobs—paid or unpaid—that you have done in your life.

My work history

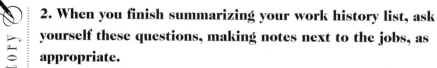

My work history

2. When you finish summarizing your work history list, ask yourself these questions, making notes next to the jobs, as appropriate.

❀ Was the salary commensurate with the work? Were you over or under paid, or not paid at all?

❀ Did you enjoy the work?

❀ What was your motivation for doing the work?

❀ Is there a pattern to your work history that stands out for you?

❀ Is there any sense of call in this history?

❀ Did you make independent decisions based on your own judgment? Or did you pursue a career because you thought you were supposed to?

❀ Did you ever create your own job?

❀ Have you ever seen a need and designed a way to fill it?

My spiritual history . . .

Certainly a key part of who we are is what we believe in, what motivates us on an inner level. Here are four questions to help you take a look at your spiritual history.

1. When did your yearning for spirituality begin?

2. Where has that yearning taken you? Exploration of different faiths? In-depth study of your original or family faith?

My spiritual history

My spiritual history

3. What, if any, life-changing spiritual experiences, insights, or dilemmas have you experienced?

4. What issues of life have you explored through the lens of faith?

Key points . . .

Take another moment and summarize for yourself any key points that have emerged as you have reviewed your work history and your spiritual history:

My Work History

1.

2.

3.

My Spiritual History

1.

2.

3.

My summary

Being in a receptive mode . . .

Grace is an active principle. I think of grace in action as being gracious to myself and to all who present themselves into my day. I define graciousness as being in a receptive mode. Graciousness isn't a synonym for "nice." Rather it is about being relaxed, anticipating good, releasing the need to feel I have to defend myself against the world. When I'm in a gracious mode, my shoulders don't tense, my back doesn't hurt.

Living in a receptive mode means never deeming a time in your life as "outside the plan" or insignificant. It means accepting each stage of growth as important.

Graciousness means holding your hand open rather than walking around with a clenched fist. It means answering the doorbell with a receptivity to whomever might be calling instead of arriving at the door irritated at being bothered. It means the difference between feeling welcomed and feeling you have interrupted people when you walk into their home.

Living in a receptive mode means never deeming a time in your life as "outside the plan" or insignificant. It means accepting each stage of growth as important. It means being open to hearing the call to what is important.

There is so much "noise" in the lives of people in industrialized countries: commitments, work, family, television, computers, radios, advertisements, reading material, telephones, cell phones, pagers, vacations. How can we possibly hear a spiritual call in the midst of all this?

To hear your call over the din of daily demands, you need to allow yourself to be in a listening posture, in a receptive mode. Many women I know have built silence into their routines a few mornings a week or part of one day each month. One thing I do know: To make silence happen in your life, you need to put it on your calendar. Silence doesn't usually happen by accident.

When you are silent, ask yourself: What am I hearing today? Be open. Let the answers come, now or later. You don't need to force them; they have their own energy. As women, we seem to be always trying to do so much. Don't DO… BE. And you will begin to feel the motion of direction.

Paying attention . . .

Although some people may describe their "call" as coming in a lightning-bolt or stunning revelation, for most of us, call comes one step at a time, bit by bit. We have a sense, we pursue an interest, and in due time, our call begins to take shape.

I think of Beth Eliason, a woman whom I met by chance at a conference—even though a mutual friend had been trying to get us together for months. Beth had always felt a strong pull to the culture and language of China. Her attraction persisted through marriage, being a mother, doing community service, and going back to college. In the course of her explorations, she saw a video of a convent in China. When she later took a trip to China with a Waterbury, Connecticut chorale, it happened that one of the tour guides was a student of the Superior of the order of Buddhist nuns she had seen on the video. That guide helped set Beth's dream in motion, and she is now going to teach English as a second language to the very same convent of Buddhist nuns she had seen in the video. Exceeding even her wildest expectations, she has been asked by the Superior of the convent to be a bridge between Buddhism and Christianity. By paying attention to her interest, by allowing herself to follow the thread that emerged, Beth is living out her dream.

What calls to you? . . .

A call can come through a talent, a strong desire, an urge, or a notion. We often see a call in motion in a singer, dancer, ball player, swimmer, or an artist. We most often notice call in another when they forsake the usual path and embark on a new path with risks, or pursue an idea that goes counter to prevailing attitudes.

A call can be an embracing of what is truly available rather than a quest for what's more and different.

Call can also be seen in the motion of daily living. The desire to stay home to raise children rather than leave the home to work... the interest in making a healthy meal several nights a week rather than eating out of a box... the quiet resolve to scour the shelves of the local library to find pleasing or inspiring books... the goal to live a life of harmony just where you are, surrounded and supported by small signs of peace—a lighted candle, a warm soup, a hearty laugh.

In talking with people about their search for their call, I recommend thinking simple. Sometimes in the quest for more money to buy more things, we reject the beauty of the rhythm of life as it can be lived even in the twenty-first century. A call can be an embracing of what is truly available rather than a quest for what's more and different.

Take some time now to write down what you are sensing for yourself as you focus on this idea of call. You may have just a fragment or small bit of an idea. You may simply be aware of an image or feeling. As you write, let yourself be receptive to whatever comes to you, without judgment or qualifiers, without weighing the pros and cons, the reality vs. the possibility.

My call

Recap . . .

In this chapter you have opened yourself up to some dreams and possibilities. There is one more thing I am going to ask of you—to do nothing. Yes... you read this correctly. Do nothing. Just sit and let your thoughts come to you.

Women are familiar with slow growth. Let this be a time of gestation. This is not the time to hurry yourself or demand a plan. This is the time to hold your thoughts quietly, until a clearer vision forms, to nurture your new thoughts. Hold them in a sacred space until they begin to grow and change. Allow them to unfold in their own time.

Allow your curiosity to just see what takes shape. And create space to let new ideas enter, to take hold and grow.

Let your imagination be active. Daydream. As a child, I was told not to daydream, as though it were a bad thing. Now I know that daydreaming is an active ingredient of hearing inner direction.

Pay attention to your nighttime dreams, too. You might want to record them in your journal. When you reread them, it may be easier to hear the messages encoded in your images.

Let your answers to the questions asked of you in this book flow through the silence into your soul's time and space.

Chapter Six

Your Action Plan

The eighth day of creation . . .

I believe we are living in the "eighth day of creation." This is a concept used by Elizabeth O'Connor that means creation continues, and that we are the co-creators of ourselves and the future world. We have the responsibility of not just enjoying creation, but of encouraging its unfolding.

As O'Connor has written, "If we are to make ultimate sense of our lives, all the disparate elements in us have to be integrated around call." The element of money is no exception. I believe that money is a gift, along with the many other resources given in different form and measure to each of us.

And I believe that the money you need to pursue your divine path, to achieve your deepest desires, to work for the good of others, is available and can be accessed, albeit in unusual or unexpected ways.

The Money Journey Circle

"Call has many facets because the whole of life coheres around it.

If we are to make ultimate sense of our lives, all the disparate elements in us have to be integrated around call."

—*Elizabeth O'Connor,*
CRY PAIN, CRY HOPE

You have begun a money journey that will keep evolving over time. You started with your financial history: your MONEY MESSAGES and your MONEY AUTOBIOGRAPHY. You moved to recognizing your MONEY FACTS & FEELINGS and creating ALIGNMENT. And you have considered some of your DREAMS. You are now ready to move to the sixth stage of The Money Journey Circle: taking ACTION. This is the time to walk into your future by taking specific steps.

Using money consciously . . .

Taking action grows out of knowing what is important to you and deciding how you will use your means toward the ends you truly desire. The actions you decide to take may not be big ones. What I am talking about is a consciousness of what you have and what you care about.

For example, I don't think I need another sheet or towel in my life. But each time I see those "white sales" advertised, I want to run out and buy more, at half price. It's a habit, it's something my family and friends often do. And maybe they need the sheets, but I don't. Instead, I can stop and decide whether that $50, $75, $100 could be used with far more satisfaction. What if I were to give it as a gift to someone who needs it? Or contribute it to a community activity? Or invest it in another share of stock? Or buy a theater ticket to a play I wanted to see but felt I couldn't afford?

You may be wondering, "Do I have to put my economic needs aside for the sake of compassion for others?" I think you have to take care of yourself in order to take care of others. Using your money consciously can resolve the conflicts in your heart as well as in your pocketbook.

"What does the Lord require of you but to do justice, and to love kindness and to walk humbly with your God?"
– Micah 6:8-9

One of my joys is to send greeting cards. Even when I was divorced with five kids, three of whom were in college, I used to come home some days with $20 worth of greeting cards. It was a real eye-opener to me when I learned how to create my own cards at far less expense. I could still send a message of love, sympathy, or congratulations—but at far less cost. This kind of shift has happened over and over in my life, thanks to a growing awareness of acting out of what is important to me.

I now use the library more rather than buying books; I get together with friends without the expense of entertaining or restaurants and have the fun of potluck suppers instead.

When we act out of misalignment, we're left with a feeling that there is never enough money. I think satisfaction eludes us because we don't even know where satisfaction comes from, and so we try to satisfy the dictates of other influences. Satisfaction comes from tapping into our core—spirit, soul, psyche, heart, intention—and from knowing our material resources and using them wisely and intentionally.

The thrilling part of acting out of financial and spiritual alignment is that, rather than putting a painful restriction on spending, it is a liberating experience of reaching for what you want by using what you have.

Vision . . .

I believe that the way we spend money does make a difference. The very act of using money is a vote, a voice creating a powerful vibration in our own lives and beyond. It reaches the political arena, the manufacturing and service sectors, our houses of worship, schools and universities, and the direction of our family life and our communities.

By adding our vision as women, we are completing what, until now in many societies, has been mainly a male-oriented vision. Our voice, our choices, our actions, and yes, our money, is needed for the fullness of the world. How much we as women can contribute!

Salespeople, advertisers, product designers, market researchers all know about the power of the woman as consumer, and they are hard at work redirecting our money to their ends. They serve as a wake-up call to remind us that there is plenty of competition for our dollars.

The materialistic focus of our society simply makes it that much harder to make choices that are in line with who we really are and what we want to create. With all the noise of the external communicators, it can be almost impossible at times to hear the still, small voice of our inner messenger.

> *"Woman . . . daring to think and move and speak—to undertake to help shape, mold and direct the thought of her age, is merely completing the circle of the world's vision."*
>
> —Anna Julia Cooper, *A VOICE FROM THE SOUTH, 1892*

Bringing our financial values and our spiritual vision together means understanding our resources and being intentional about our choices. It allows us to operate from a place of fulfillment so we have the energy not just to make our own lives hum, but to contribute to the possibilities of others.

Such is the case with the Holly Wheeler Fund. You've never heard of that fund? I'm not surprised. It was started by a friend of mine... for herself. Holly and I were sitting on the beach one day as she talked about wanting to go back to school for training as a psychotherapist. But—and this may sound very familiar—she didn't have the money.

I replied, "Why don't you ask friends and family to help you?"

Her immediate response was, "Oh, I can't do that."

And I said, "Of course you can." And I gave her a check for ten dollars to begin the Holly Fund.

Now that contribution was not going to pay for her education, but it did serve to jump-start her ability to get to school. I was so inspired by her enthusiasm to begin a new career that I made a gesture. And in that gesture, she saw the possibility that somehow, from somewhere, the money would come if she followed her dream.

I recently got a letter from Holly in which she said, "I would never have taken the plunge without your 'of course you can do this' encouragement." She has applied to the institute that she is interested in attending and is pursuing the Holly Fund as a creative way to generate the money she needs.

I think we all have the ability to listen, to take a step, and to empower people. It doesn't take much. Even ten dollars will do. One woman, working with others, using the money available to her… creating far-reaching action and opportunities. Who knows what can spring from such efforts, and when?

Getting clearer . . .

Have you ever written a "mission statement" for yourself? Before you let those words intimidate you, think of it this way: "If I could transform just one small bit of my current reality—or the whole thing—what might I be ready to do? Or what I might be ready to *begin* to *think* about doing?"

The core of your mission is what is important to you. It might be to bring comfort to an elderly relative on a weekly basis. Or to do something to address the problem of homelessness in your city. Or to create peace and stability in your own home. Don't let your mission be determined by what another person expects of you, or what you expect from yourself from a previous time in your life. This is a whole new era in your life. Give yourself some time to consider these next two questions:

What are some specific things that are important to you at this time in your life?

My priorities

What actions could you take to make these things begin to happen? (Scheduling in a visit to a nursing home? Learning the bus route to get there? Or petitioning your city representative to consider legislation for homeless relief? Contributing to an organization that works with homeless people? Or cutting back on your activities? Introducing one "quiet night" each week?)

Possibilities . . .

Any action plan ultimately needs some specifics, some clear intention to carry it out. But you do not need elaborate plans. Consider specific small changes you might make to get clearer about your call. Here are some decisions other women have told me they have made to get clarity:

- ✿ I will carry a small memo pad with me and make notes in it about my daily financial activities: spending, financial decisions, and feelings.

- ✿ I will meditate for 5 minutes, starting at 7 a.m., every day for one week. I will follow my meditation with 5 minutes of journaling about what is next for me on my money journey. Each Sunday morning I will spend 15 minutes reviewing my journal.

- ✿ I will check out a debtors anonymous meeting because I see a problem with debt in my financial picture.

- ✿ I will designate the next four Wednesday nights as "Quiet Nights." There will be no TV or music or computers turned on. I will read or write about my financial concerns and interests.

- ✿ I will start a money and spirituality group at my church.

- ✿ I will give $50 to something I find I have passion about, just to see how I feel doing it. I will make notes in my journal about my feelings.

❀ I will join an investment club.

❀ I will interview a financial planner to help me with the actions I would like to take.

❀ I will check out the possibility of taking a continuing education course in finances at the local college.

❀ I will try out a computer software program that will help me keep track of bills and checks.

❀ I will change one financial behavior: For the next month, instead of buying gourmet coffee every morning, I will save that money to give to someone who could use a little help right now.

❀ I will check out the business and finance rack at a bookstore and look for publications that are in tune with my needs and interests.

❀ I will go to the library for the next two Thursday evenings from 6 to 7:30 to research information about homeless people in my city. I will record what I read and journal about my feelings. I will make this commitment in my calendar and let nothing interfere.

❀ I will continue to pray for guidance in my financial life.

My next step

What will your next steps be? Make some promises to yourself about what you will do to move forward on your money journey and note them here.

Write down the name of one person whom you will share these plans with—someone to whom you can be accountable for carrying them out.

"Bag lady" . . .

Just the words "bag lady" can inspire fear. In my experience in discussing money and call with women, I have seen over and over again that, at this stage of "getting real" about possible choices and changes, money fears seem to rise again to the top of the list: How much it will cost? Can I earn enough if I do that? Will I have enough money if I make that choice? Will I end up a "bag lady"?

These types of "bag lady" fears influence many women: the idea that somehow, if we take charge of our money, if we make choices that follow our heart, we will lose everything and end up on the street in rags, pushing a shopping cart filled with our only belongings. Homelessness is surely an extreme and very sad part of our society, but it is not a likely result for anyone who is seriously coming to grips with finances. Trust me. It's not going to happen. You are going to move slowly. You are going to take things one step at a time.

I do know this: "Bag lady" fears surface most often when money—or the lack of it—is the top priority. And as long as you put money concerns at the head of your list, you will block your path. Your fears will get in the way of the possibilities available to you. It is important to come to grips with your fears about money in order to hear your call clearly.

Consider what you are afraid of. Success? Failure? Being alone? Losing a job? Losing money? Losing the love of a family member? Losing someone's respect? Being sick? War? Fire? Economic downturn? Dying? Someone else dying? Being criticized?

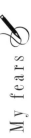

My fears

Write down any money fears that come to mind. Don't hold back on just what might be keeping you from moving forward.

I am afraid of...

Now write down your money fears again, uncensored. Yes, you just did that, but I want you to try again. The first time around you may have filtered out some fears. Remember, fears limit you. Naming your fears may well unlock paralysis in some areas of your life.

I am afraid of...

My fears

Keep on keeping on . . .

Sue Roselle did not become penniless when she gave up her high-powered job and returned to Pittsburgh. She found work and a lifestyle in a community that resonated with her spirit.

Anne Hastings did not let the external obstacles of Father Fillipe's lack of funds stop her from moving to Haiti, helping start a bank, and finding a deeper meaning for her life.

> *"Any good that I may do, let me do it now, as I may not pass this way again."*
>
> *—an old saying my mother used to tell me*

To fulfill her dream of becoming a chiropractor, Sharon Williams did not give up when there was no apparent money to fund her education. She used borrowed money to achieve her goal of helping people heal, and her success is allowing her to pay back her debt.

To fund the dreams of others through providing seed money, Charlotte Fardelmann did not dispose of her inherited wealth. She took a portion of it and put it together with the contributions of others.

What is the message here? Don't let your fears block your possibilities.

Feelings about money are internal territory not often discussed because we feel uncomfortable, and these untouched fears can be like unexploded land mines. The potential is there to do you harm if you don't dig them out and release them. Clearing up a minefield can turn it into a field of possibilities.

One way to move beyond your fears is to talk about them with your friends and allow your fears to be more vocal and visible. If you have been working in a group as you've gone through the processes in this book, use the members as a sounding board. Or confide in a friend whom you can trust.

Above all, be patient with yourself. Be kind to yourself. Compliment yourself. You are doing a good job. Keep it up. Made a mistake? Do it over or just go on. Mistakes are part of the pattern of our lives. Let go of remorse and guilt. Acknowledge how you feel and go on. That is the important part: Keep on keeping on.

A psalm for midwives . . .

This last section of the book has focused on the wide variety of ways in which women have identified their dreams, heard a call, and taken action to begin a new life's work. You have been asked to become aware of the presence of dreams in your life, and you are being challenged to take the next step.

The action stage of your money journey is a stage of vulnerability. As you explore new ideas and experiment with new actions, you will be taking risks. You may face new challenges, you may get discouraged, you may experience times of excitement. As you move forward, on your journey, hold this thought in your mind: As I birth my dreams into actions, I am midwifing my future.

The metaphor of midwife has always had special resonance for women and is beautifully expressed in the following psalm by Miriam Therese Winter, a member of the Medical Mission Sisters in Hartford, Connecticut, who is well-known as a song writer, author, and leader in feminist spirituality. Read it slowly and take it to heart for your journey.

A Psalm for Midwives
by Miriam Therese Winter

Choir 1

You will know
when it is time
to bring to birth
the new creation.

Choir 2

The signs
will be all around you,
urging, insisting:
now is the time.

Choir 1

You have to know
just when to bear down
and concentrate
on one thing only.

Choir 2

It takes labor,
hard, hard labor
to bring forth something new.

All

Be Midwife to our dreams,
Shaddai.
Make midwives of us all.

Choir 1

You have to know
just when to push
for something that is
worth fighting for.

Choir 2

If you push too soon,
the dream,
so close to fulfillment,
may be stillborn.

Choir 1

You have to know
how hard to push
when something new
is about to happen.

Choir 2

If you push too hard,
you may be too exhausted
or too discouraged
to continue on,
or someone may step in
to stop you,
causing you to abort.

All
Be Midwife to our hopes,
Shaddai.
Make midwives of us all.

Choir 1
You have to know
how to cut the cord
and how to let go
of what has been;

Choir 2
for what will be
will be different
and it will take some time
to adjust.

Choir 1
You have to know
how to wait
for things to settle
after the dream is born,

Choir 2
and how to handle
the consequences—
clean up the mess
and then move on.

All
Be Midwife to our freedom,
Shaddai.
Make midwives of us all.

Choir 1
How good it is
to bring to birth.

Choir 2
or to help another
bring to birth.

Choir 1
How good it is
to deliver the dream.

Choir 2
Let us nurture it
to fulfillment.

All
Be Midwife to the future,
Shaddai.
Make midwives of us all.

(Note: in this song, the word Shaddai comes from the Hebrew and is considered a name for the female aspect of God, sometimes translated as "the breasted one.")

Moving forward . . .

As I finish writing this book, I am also experiencing my reactions from my latest trip to Haiti. I spent time there with the women of Cite Soleil, a neighborhood slum built on a garbage dump, with open sewage canals running through it. I also stayed with the women of Fondwa, a village in the mountains. The faces of these women keep showing up on the inner screen of my mind. I know they want the same things for themselves and their children that I do.

I am unsettled by their reality juxtaposed to the prosperity enjoyed by many people around the world. Why is there such inequity? And what can I do about it? I cannot simply reenter my life in the United States without thinking about the poor women of the world who have no welfare, public health, or education systems. No cushion of safety exists to provide even the most basic necessities of food and medicine to those who need them most.

Despite the most difficult conditions, I watch people try to survive as best they can. In Haiti and other countries, the women band together to help each other, sharing their small measure of food, or pooling their little bit of money to buy medicine for one of their children who is sick.

As I listen to the questions from so many women in the United States about what can they do with their lives and their resources, I feel a renewal of my inspiration and my commitment to answer my call: to make a bridge between women here and women in Haiti and other countries. I imagine the possibilities of creating new programs in addition to the projects we've begun with the help of other women in Haiti and Bosnia.

In my dreams, I see an "Adopt A Mother" program as a way for women to reach out to other women, one-on-one. How little it would take in money to make a big difference in a Haitian woman's life! And what a small financial, but large spiritual, contribution it would be in the lives of affluent women. No big organizations or administrative costs... just one woman "adopting" another, sharing resources and love.

Yet much would have to be done to create "Adopt A Mother." Many people, plans, and commitments would be needed. The experience of call is not like one-stop shopping. It is a life-engaging process with its own momentum. It does not exclude the other pleasures and activities of life, but it does have a core place in your purpose here on earth and is ever-evolving.

If you worry about money, about how things will work out in your life, you are just being human. But in doing the work of this book, I hope you have experienced another reality too: You don't need to let those worries rule your life. You can work with your history, your current facts, and your deepest soul motivations to mold your life in a different way. And when you have those moments of doubt about the hard facts of reality versus the soft murmuring of the soul, recall these brief words of Ada Maria Isasi-Diaz, a Latina theologian, author, and teacher:

> *"The only way we can move forward
> is to live the reality we envision."*

"The only way we can move forward is to live the reality we envision."

—Ada Maria Isasi-Diaz,
from the Sister Fund
Annual Report

Resources . . . you!

One of the most valuable resources you have is … YOU. Before you close this book, give honor to your process by taking the time to write a summary of your learning and your commitment. As you move on, you can refer to this summary, revise it, use it for meditation, and develop it as a basis for further action.

My journey

Important money messages I have identified that have influenced my thinking and behavior:

Important facts from my money autobiography that have influenced my decisions:

My current financial facts are:

    Assets   _____

    Liabilities   _____

    Net Worth   _____

My most recent cash flow reflects:

    Income   _____

    Expenditures   _____

    Net Cash Flow   _____

At the moment, my life work is focused on:

My journey

I express my current spiritual life as follows:

The things that feed my soul are:

I am passionate about:

Organizations or projects I would like to support include:

My plans:

Direction(s) I want to keep:

Things I want to change:

My journey

Questions or topics I would like to revisit periodically:

Recap . . .

Your personal summary of your MONEY MESSAGES, your MONEY AUTOBIOGRAPHY, your MONEY FACTS & FEELINGS, the ALIGNMENT with your spiritual vision, your DREAMS, and your ACTIONS can be a valuable tool. Make plans to review it on a periodic basis.

One system that works for some people is to review it on their birthday, anniversary, or other important personal date. Along with the usual rituals of those days, you might want to create a ritual of looking at this summary and updating it, taking into account who you are at that moment in time.

If you have been working with this book in a group, consider scheduling periodic meetings where you can share your updates with the other members. You might also want to consider a project that you could do together. By now, you have shared your fears and dreams in a way that few others have. Use that energy to create something new.

Or you might want to take the work that you have done in this book into the world by creating a Money Journey Circle for other women. Circles have always been very important among women throughout the world. If you want to start such a circle, I suggest you refer to Jean Shinoda Bolen's book *The Millionth Circle.*

Clearly your money journey does not end with the end of this book. Here are some ideas about ways you can continue your journey:

❀ Experiment shifting direction by spending your money in a different way, gradually.

❀ Use some of the thoughts you have written as a source for personal meditation.

❀ Become more conscious of your day-to-day transactions by observing, gently, on a regular basis, how you respond to money issues.

❀ Ask yourself some open-ended questions. For example, "What do I need to do about my financial life?"

A parting gift . . .

Regardless of where your dreams take you, I hope you have completed this book with a new and deep appreciation for your history, your resources, your power, and your faith.

In closing, I want to offer you the Spiritual Money Journey chart on the facing page. You might want to post it in a place where you can refer to it often as you continue your money journey. It can serve as a source of encouragement, reminding you of your goals, and keeping you in touch with the reasons why you embarked on this money journey in the first place.

Remember: Every possibility is open to you.

My Spiritual Money Journey

❀ To see money as one of the gifts in my life.

❀ To recognize the difference between my needs and my wants.

❀ To stay clear about my "response-ability" in relation to the money I have earned, inherited, or been given.

❀ To pray and reflect on what I truly want to do with that money.

❀ To clarify how I will share, use, save, invest, or spend that money wisely.

❀ To base my financial decisions on my inner voice, rather than a message from the past.

❀ To be aware of whose agenda I am following: mine or someone else's or God's.

❀ To view my use of money in the context of my whole life, keeping my financial transactions in alignment with my spiritual values.

Ending prayer . . .

O Birther of Dreams, Source of Creative Energy, I give thanks that you supply confidence when I face doubts, hope when I despair, strength when I feel weak, courage when I want to give in to conventional wisdom, and faith when I can no longer pray.

I praise you that you provide resources through people, places, and things. I pray for integrity and faithfulness to keep focused on the vision and mindful of the need for both depth and breadth, reflection and action, justice and prayers.

Through your boundless grace and faithful care, you have walked with me to bring to term my fledgling dreams and to make of them a place of renewal and healing and a work worthy of your blessing. I give you thanks in the Name of our Creator God who continues to birth new life and new possibility.

—Ruth Halvorson, former director of the ARC
Retreat Center, Stanchfield, Minnesota

Other resources . . .

BOOKS

The Call to the Soul, Marjory Zoet Bankson (Philadelphia: Innisfree Press, 1999).
> An excellent resource on the exploration of call as it relates to spiritual development.

Inspired Philanthropy, Tracy Gary, Melissa Kohner, Nancy Adess (Berkeley: Chardon Press, 1998).
> A workbook designed to help you find your passion and to identify ways to personally make philanthropic contributions.

A Woman's Journey to God: Finding the Feminine Path, Joan Borysenko (New York: Riverhead Books, 1999).
> Stories about women's ways to the spiritual life.

Harold and the Purple Crayon, Crockett Johnson (New York: HarperCollins Juvenile Books, 1981).
> A children's story about a little boy who uses a purple crayon to draw his life, and what he draws becomes real. A wonderful way to bring the quality of imagination back into your life.

The Path: Creating Your Mission Statement for Work and for Life, Laurie Beth Jones (New York: Hyperion, 1996).
> A simplified way to define your life's mission and develop a clear declaration.

The Vein of Gold, Julia Cameron (New York: Jeremy P. Tarcher, 1997).
> Expanding on the idea of a spiritual DNA, Cameron offers the reader a way to explore and elicit the emergence of their own creativity.

The Millionth Circle: How to Change Ourselves and the World,
Jean Shinoda Bolen (Berkeley, CA: Conari Press, 1999).

> Dr. Bolen wrote this book "to inspire women to form circles." She believes that the movement to form women's circles will change the world and bring humanity into a post-patriarchal era.

Nudged by the Spirit: Stories of People Responding to the Still, Small Voice of God, Charlotte Fardelmann (Pendle Hill, PA: Pendle Hill Publications, 2001).

> Stories of the dreams that have come to fruition with the help of seed money from the Lyman Fund.

MAGAZINES

YES
Positive Futures Network
PO Box 10818
Bainbridge Island, WA 98110

> A magazine designed especially to tell stories of good and creative events in the world—truly good news.

Hope
PO Box 160
Brooklin, ME 04616

> A magazine that seeks to inspire a sense of hope by celebrating individuals and organizations that are working to make the world a better place.

Lapis
Published by the New York Open Center, Inc.
83 Spring St
New York, NY 10012
212-334-0210
>   A magazine concerned with the inner meaning of
>   contemporary life.

Faith @ Work Magazine
Faith at Work
106 E. Broad Street
Falls Church, VA 22046-4501
703-237-3426
www.FaithAtWork.com
>   A magazine with practical information about faith,
>   family, community, and worklife.

STUDY GROUPS

Institute of Noetic Sciences
475 Gate Five Road, Ste 300
Sausalito, CA 94965-0909
415-331-5673
www.noetic.org
>   Their journal chronicles trends, new ideas, and data
>   in the interdisciplinary field of conscious research.

Marion Foundation
3 Barnabas Road
Marion, MA 02738-1421
508-748-0816
www.marionfoundation.org
> An organization providing workshops and a monthly mailing about philanthropy, alternative medicine, and global spiritual and economic concerns.

Women of Vision
1651 East 4th Street, Suite 229
Santa Ana, CA 92701
714-547-9570
> Women of Vision, a program of World Vision, seeks to educate and motivate women to become women of action who invest their time, minds, compassion, creativity, and finances to make a personal difference in this world.

INTERFAITH GROUPS

Ministry of Money
11315 Neelsville Church Rd
Germantown, MD 20876
800-275-6585
www.ministryofmoney.org
> For over 25 years, Ministry of Money has provided opportunities for people to explore their relationship to money from a faith perspective. They offer weekend retreats, pilgrimages to developing countries, a quarterly newsletter and special-topic one-day workshops to help people continue on their faith and money journeys.

Women's Perspective
421 Meadow Street
Fairfield, CT 06430
203-336-2238
www.womensperspective.org

The Women's Perspective offers retreats and
workshops on the subject of spirituality and money in
various locations in the United States as well as
transitional travel workshops to third world
countries.

United Religions Initiative
PO Box 29242
San Francisco, CA 94129
415-561-2300

This organization promotes interfaith cooperation
through their website, a newsletter, conferences, and
the development of worldwide cooperation circles.

Index

ROSEMARY C. WILLIAMS is the director of the Women's Perspective. In this capacity she designs and conducts retreats and workshops across the country on the subject of money and spirituality, and leads transformational trips to countries suffering economic deprivation. As a financial planner and former banker, she has combined her professional training with her faith. This synthesis of financial know-how and spiritual belief has led her to participate in the initiation of community development projects in Haiti. She lives in Connecticut and is the mother of five grown children.

JOANNE KABAK is a Connecticut-based journalist who writes about personal finance, health and contemporary lifestyles. She is published in newspapers, magazines and on the Web. Prior to becoming a writer and editor, she earned her MBA degree at Columbia University and practiced as a CPA in New York City.

About Women's Perspective . . .

The Women's Perspective scheduled its first events in the early 1980s in recognition of the fact that women brought a unique voice to the subjects of money, faith, and economic justice. We continue to design and facilitate retreats and workshops that provide space for women to explore their relationship with money. We offer a safe place to learn, think, journal, and examine the impact money has on our faith, self image, family, relationships, and community.

In addition to retreats and workshops, we offer transformational trips to economically deprived countries, such as Haiti and India. On these trips we develop relationships with women of the country we visit in order to understand their lives and share our friendship, experiences, and resources. Through the generosity of the Hardin Generativity Trust and individual donors, we have started several initiatives. These include: economic partnerships with women's groups in Haiti, the establishment of two community radio stations, advanced educational opportunities for a few Haitian women, marketing the products of an embroidery cooperative, and ongoing financial support for a small health clinic. We have nurtured many friendships across the cultural boundaries of our countries and continue to transform our own lives as well as those of the women we meet in our travels.

As we deepen our commitment to working with the issues of money and spirituality, we encourage women to come together in small circles to continue sharing their experiences related to money, faith, and values.

To get more information, register for a retreat, or become part of a local group, you can reach us in the following ways:

On the Web: www.womensperspective.org
By phone: 203-336-2238
By fax: 203-336-2240
By email: rwilli7994@att.net, wpromar@hotmail .com
By mail: 421 Meadow St., Fairfield, CT 06430

Innisfree Classics that Call to the Deep Heart's Core

The Call to the Soul
Six Stages of Spiritual Development
by Marjory Zoet Bankson

Circle of Stones
Woman's Journey to Herself
by Judith Duerk

Red Fire
A Quest for Awakening
by Paula D'Arcy

The Circle Continues
Women Respond to Circle of Stones
Gathered by Judith Duerk

Leading Ladies
Transformative Biblical Images for Women's Leadership
by Jeanne L. Porter, Ph.D.

Return to the Sea
Reflections on Anne Morrow Lindbergh's GIFT FROM THE SEA
by Anne M. Johnson
Foreword by Reeve Lindbergh

Sabbath Sense
A Spiritual Antidote for the Overworked
by Donna Schaper

The Tao of Eating
Feeding Your Soul Through Everyday Experiences with Food
by Linda R. Harper, Ph.D.
Foreword by Thomas Moore

Call for Our Free Complete Catalog
1-800-367-5872
Find Innisfree books in your local bookstore.

Innisfree Press, Inc.
136 Roumfort Road
Philadelphia, PA
19119-1632

www.InnisfreePress.com